palaces for the people/
prefabs in post-war britain

For everyone who fought to save their prefab from premature demolition

palaces for the people/
prefabs in post-war britain
greg stevenson

batsford/

/Greg Stevenson

All rights reserved. No part of this publication may be reproduced in any form without written permission from the publisher / A CIP record for this book is available from the British Library / First published 2003 by B T Batsford / 64 Brewery Road / London N7 9NT / www.batsford.com / Design Claudia Schenk / Copyright © 2003 Greg Stevenson / ISBN 0 7134 8823 9 / Printing in Italy

contents/

- 7/ **Preface**
- 11/ **Introduction**
- 25/ **Building the new Jerusalem**
- 55/ **The Temporary Housing Programme**
- 103/ **Prefab interiors**
- 137/ **Prefab life**
- 191/ **Permanent prefabs**
- 217/ **Epilogue**
- 232/ **Places to visit**
- 235/ **Bibliography**
- 240/ **Picture credits**

preface/

Prefabricated homes were intended to be a temporary answer to Britain's housing crisis after World War 2. With ample light and space, and providing an instant sense of identity and community, these 'palaces for the people' came to be perhaps our best-loved post-war architecture.

The continuing shortage of housing in the decades after the war, and campaigns by prefab residents to save their homes, ensured that hundreds of these bungalows survived to more than five times their intended lifespan. In tracing the surviving examples, following campaigns to save prefabs from demolition, and interviewing the last of the prefab residents I soon realised that this was the last opportunity to record the story. Aside from the handful that have been protected by listing or reconstructed as museums, virtually all the remaining Temporary Housing Programme prefabs in Britain are currently under threat of demolition. Hundreds were destroyed while I prepared my research; soon only a few dozen will remain. It was this wholesale destruction that compelled me to undertake this work – to present the histories of these 'curious huts' to the generations to come.

This book does not provide a technical description of prefabrication, nor is it a history of the planning process that led to the construction of 156,623 temporary homes between 1945 and 1949. These are provided elsewhere.[1] Instead this book introduces post-war British prefabs, their interiors, and the lives of their residents. It concentrates on the bungalows erected under the Temporary Housing Programme, and introduces some of the antecedents and successors of that exciting era in the history of British homes.

1/ Mary Valente and family standing proudly in front of their first home, an Arcon Mark V in Selly Park, Birmingham (1947).

Acknowledgements

Knocking on the doors of the remaining prefab estates, I never ceased to be amazed by the helpfulness of the residents, many who had remained in their humble home since the late 1940s. Sincere thanks to all who answered my questions about prefab life, or wrote to me with photographs and memories.

Authors Gary Robins, Brenda Vale, and journalist Clive Fewins have been very generous with their time and knowledge. Thanks also to Elain Harwood at English Heritage, Gerallt Nash at the Museum of Welsh Life, Phil Thoms at Newport Housing Trust, Ian Leith at the National Monuments Record, and Marguerite Patten who kindly let me reproduce one of her ration recipes.

At Batsford I am indebted to Tom Neville for his enthusiasm for the project, and Claudia Schenk for her design work. Special thanks go to my parents for scanning many of the old photographs, and to Martin for his patience.

Greg Stevenson, Lampeter, February 2003

---

[1] See the excellent books by R B White (1965) and Brenda Vale (1995).

2/ Mrs Rhys John preparing bread and butter pudding in her Arcon kitchen. In the alcove above her stand the coronation tea plates that were given to residents of all the prefabs on her estate (1953).

How very little, since things were made,
Things have altered in the building trade.
Rudyard Kipling, 'A Truthful Song'

Factory-built prefabricated houses that provided 'instant' homes in the years immediately after World War 2 captured the imagination of the British people. As Prime Minister Winston Churchill's proposed solution to the dire housing shortage, prefabricated bungalows attracted the attention of a public keen to know what would be done to satisfy their need for accommodation. Whether people commented with disdain on the impersonal uniformity of these 'chicken sheds' or with excitement at the prospect of a new way of living, prefabricated homes that could be erected in a matter of hours became indelibly linked with the reconstruction effort in the national consciousness.

The abbreviation 'prefab' was soon adopted as a label for the thousands of quirky bungalows that sprouted in the suburbs of most large towns. The term has since become a catch-all phrase used to describe any building that has largely been prefabricated before final construction. Such a loose definition encompasses everything from houses that arrived virtually complete on the back of a truck, to system-built houses that required all cladding to be added at the construction site. Of the post-war prefabs only the Aluminium Bungalow was wholly prefabricated, and most were versions of steel or timber frames with asbestos or concrete cladding. The 'prefab' name has stuck, and now encompasses all 13 house types built under the 1944 Temporary Housing Pro-

3/ A 1920s prefab home with asbestos roof in rural Ceredigion, still providing a comfortable home after 80 years.

introduction/

gramme, and indeed many built later. The very fact that the general public adopted the technical term is an indication of the success of Churchill's publicity machine that promised a quarter of a million temporary prefab homes. In the event, less than 160,000 homes were constructed under the programme, but the idea of a house that could be mass-produced in a factory caught the imagination of the public, and today we talk about prefabs as a generic label rather than 'temps' (for temporary homes) or the trade names chosen by manufacturers – Arcons, Spooners, Phoenixes, Tarrans, etc.

Despite their modern appearance, and the fact that they were identified by some as the homes of the future, the prefabs of the 1940s were in fact building on centuries of tradition. Prefabrication of houses in Britain dates back to the

4/ Timber-framed and cruck buildings have been prefabricated for centuries. Carpenters' marks on individual components indicate the construction technique.

fourteenth century when shepherds took portable wooden houses with them when staying on open downland. Medieval cruck and other homes of timber frame construction were virtually all prefabricated and re-erected on site. Heavy oak parts would often have holes drilled into them for fixings, and the structural elements would be numbered with a labelling system akin to Roman numerals. This allowed the housewright to deconstruct the frame, take the parts to the site, reconstruct it, and then make the walls solid with whichever material was used locally. There was even a degree of standardisation in the measurements of some timber framers, making them the first 'prefab' manufacturers.

British housing becoming increasingly standardised as the rebuilding of towns in the eighteenth and nineteenth centuries followed uniform patterns. Timber-framed 'prefabs' continued to be built into the nineteenth century in rural areas where good building stone was scarce. For the most part, however, timber-frame construction was destroyed by the navy's need for timber during the Napoleonic wars, and the subsequent introduction of cheap mass-produced bricks. However, the concept of prefabrication did not disappear as industrialists had begun to experiment with metal-frame construction. By the mid nineteenth century, steel and iron frames were being used in many large and impressive public buildings. The Crystal Palace, for example, was built in various Birmingham workshops and then re-erected in Hyde Park, London, for the Great Exhibition of 1851.[1] By this time Britain was also exporting prefabricated houses, shops and churches to Australia and the colonies, where customers could order their preferred design in wood cladding or iron sheeting from a catalogue of surprisingly diverse designs.[2] By the turn of the twentieth century prefabrication was also being considered for fixtures and fittings, and combined cooker and bath units were manufactured which can be seen as

5/ 6/

precedents for the back-to-back kitchen and bathroom plumbing of post-war prefabs.

The period immediately after World War 1 saw investigation into prefabrication as a possible solution in times of acute housing shortage. Importantly, people recognised for the first time that the lack of housing was a national issue, and something that must be addressed by central, rather than local gov-

5/ Pair of semi-detached steel prefab homes reconstructed at the Black Country Museum. Residents found they could hang pictures on the walls using magnets. 6/ Castle Bungalow, near Bideford in Devon, a 1920s prefab produced by Boulton & Paul of Norwich. Now let for holidays by the Landmark Trust. 7/ 1–8 Howell Hill, West Camel in Somerset. A 1920s experiment by Somerset architects Petter & Warren, at £513 per home they proved more expensive than standard houses. Other examples of survive near Yeovil and in Ealing, West London.

7/

ernment. The Tudor Walters report of 1918 identified an urgent need for between 300,000 and 400,000 homes.[3] There was the added problem of where to house men demobilised from the services, and these 'Homes Fit for Heroes'[4] had to meet the inflated expectations of returning soldiers. Further complicating matters was a dearth of bricks and timber, and a severe shortage of skilled labour. There were less than half the number of bricklayers available in 1920 than there had been at the start of the twentieth century.[5] The government was forced to look at alternatives to standard brick construction and there were many investigations into prefabrication in concrete, steel or timber. The government encouraged the use of steel window casements (such as those as supplied by Crittall's), and precast-concrete window surrounds and stairs. Excess steel production from World War 1 was translated into experiments in steel prefabs in the same way that excess aluminium production after World War 2 would encourage the production of aluminium homes.

From 1919 the Committee for Standardisation and New Methods of Construction considered the materials used for state housing, and also new methods of building, including prefabrication.[6] Research highlighted the virtues of what were then non-traditional building materials such as chalk, cob and pisé (earth walling). High-profile architects such as Clough Williams-Ellis, who were seldom out of the press, espoused the virtues of such building methods.[7] The Ministry of Agriculture at Amesbury erected experimental housing using cob and chalk pisé in 1920, but the technique was not revived on a larger scale, despite the fact that it demonstrated cost savings and a feasible method of construction.

Scandinavian experience in prefabrication was recognised when several hundred Swedish prefab timber houses were imported and erected on the London County Council-owned Becontree and Watling estates between 1924 and 1928. These followed a traditional Scandinavian style and were decorated externally with creosoted horizontal wood boarding. The Amalgamated Woodworkers Union called a strike and compelled the LCC to stop importing prefabricated homes. Steel prefabs such as the Weir House and the Atholl House (named after Lord Weir and the Duke of Atholl), the Telford House and the Cowieson House similarly caused problems with the building unions who feared their members would soon be out of work if the trend progressed. Ironically, these prefabs had been developed as a means of relieving severe unemployment in the Clydebank shipyards during the 1920s. Most of these homes, which had steel plates bolted on to steel or timber frames, were of conventional appearance, and were constructed in Scotland (around 2500 in 1926–27). Few of these steel homes have survived (one has been moved to the Black Country Museum in Dudley). Although the houses were prone to condensation and damp, residents found novel advantages such as being able to attach pictures to the wall with magnets. Trade union opposition put an end to their production in 1928.

Most of the proposals considered by the Committee for Standardisation and New Methods of Construction were for concrete buildings. Some, such as the Easi-form House and the No-fines Concrete House, utilised *in-situ* concrete construction. Those that used precast concrete included the Waller House (huge precast wall slabs), the Boot House (using prefabricated panels and posts; 8260 built[8]) and the Duo-Slab House (Airey and Son Ltd; about 4250 built[9]).[10] Other trade names included the Winget House, Underdown House, Dennis Poulton, Dorlonco, Dennis-Wild and Crane. A few of the different systems (including those that used precast parts) were erected at demonstration sites across Britain, including a well-publicised example at Acton, near London. Builders and other interested parties were invited to view the new way of building. By the late 1950s many of these early concrete homes were cracking and damp.

Between 1929 and the end of World War 2 comparatively few non-traditional homes were constructed in Britain. Those that were built in the 1930s were most commonly timber-framed with prefabricated timber panels from Scanhouse Ltd, and Solid Cedar Homes Ltd (a subsidiary of Tarran Industries of Hull). Many of these were built in Scotland where brick-layers were particularly scarce at the time.[11] About 2500 prefabs were imported from Sweden and at least 100 from Norway.[12] Highland Scotland even developed a tradition of

8/ pages 18–19: From a 1903 catalogue of prefab homes from William Cooper of London. These timber-framed homes clad in corrugated-iron sheets were produced from the 1850s, and many were exported to the British colonies.

WILLIAM COOPER, Ltd., 761, Old Kent Road, London, S.E.

Portable Cottage.

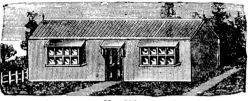

No. 619.

An attractive design, with square Bay Windows, and Porch over door. Measurements and plan of rooms as for No. 622.

For Specification, see pages 412 and 413.

Delivered to nearest Goods Station within 100 miles, and erected complete on purchaser's foundation, £62; or marked for re-erection, bundled and put on Rail or Wharf, Cash price, £44.

Portable Cottage.

No. 620.

Main structure, 28ft. by 22ft.

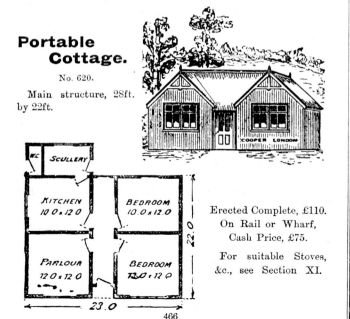

Erected Complete, £110. On Rail or Wharf, Cash Price, £75.

For suitable Stoves, &c., see Section XI.

466

WILLIAM COOPER, Ltd.,

Delivered to nearest Goods Station within 100 miles, and erected complete upon purchaser's foundation, £60; marked for re-erection, and bundled and put on rail or wharf,

Cash Price, £42.

For Specification, see pages 412 and 413.

Portable

Erected complete, £92; or

For suitable Stoves

DEAR SIR,—The structure you satisfactory. I am instructed to Yours faithfully,

WILLIAM COOPER, Ltd., 761, Old Kent Road, London, S.E.

Portable Cottage.

No. 623.

Containing three rooms and W.C. Bedroom, 12ft. by 12ft.; Sitting-room, 12ft. by 12ft.; Kitchen, 12ft. by 6ft.

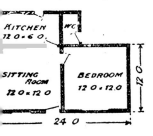

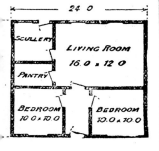

r Wharf, cash price, £62.
see Section XI.

Blackpool.
to my brother in India is very
a for careful attention to order.—
E. TURNER.

Portable Cottages.

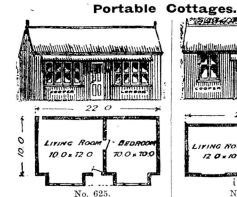

No. 625.

A two-roomed structure with square Bay. Windows and Porch.

Erected Complete, £46. On Rail or Wharf, Cash Price, £32.

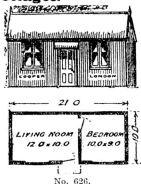

No. 626.

Another two-roomed structure with double Casement Windows and Porch.

Erected Complete, £38 10s. On Rail or Wharf, Cash Price, £27.

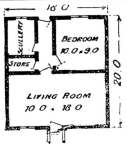

No. 627.

Erected Complete, £68. On Rail or Wharf, Cash Price, £48. For Specification, see pages 412 and 413, and for suitable Stoves, &c., see Section XI.

Erection Prices

include Delivery and Erection complete, Painting Outside Woodwork two coats best oil colour, and Staining and Varnishing Inside, Glazing Windows, &c., by our own men, all Railway Charges, Carriage, Men's Fares, Lodgings, &c., within 100 miles. Beyond this distance extra cost of Carriage, &c., will be charged.

houses built from redundant railway sleepers.[13] Prefabrication was not restricted to housing, and a few innovative prefab schools were also built during the 1930s.[14] In general, however, although there were numerous experiments into prefabrication in inter-war Britain, they were driven by the need to find a temporary solution as the building industry got back on its feet after World War 1. The lack of factory production on a large scale, and/or independent government research limited the success of prefabrication. It is likely that even those that considered prefabrication as a serious long-term solution to the British housing problem did not dare to voice their beliefs, for fear of stirring trouble with the building unions.

The 1930s saw many people enjoying improved living standards, and millions of semi-detached suburban homes cropped up all over Britain. Prices of houses fell steeply, while streamlined and cheap mortgage facilities from building societies[15] meant that young families could increasingly move out of accommodation shared with their in-laws into a home of their own. The number of cars in Britain doubled during the 1930s (to 2 million) and the new lower-middle classes found they could move out to semi-detached homes in the suburbs. Twenty million went to the cinema every week and saw the glamorous flat-roofed homes of Hollywood. With a wireless in almost every home Britain underwent a 'communications revolution', and even people in rural areas would have been aware of national and international news, as well as the latest fashions for the home.[16] Dozens of newly available magazine titles marketed to housewives – including *Good Housekeeping* and *Modern Home* – promoted the virtues of a tidy, well-designed house in the contemporary style.

Living in a detached or semi-detached home had become a reality for many people, who even found that they could afford to keep part of their garden as an area of formal display. Whereas at the beginning of the inter-war period many found themselves with no choice as to the furnishings they owned (many renting terraced accommodation), by the outbreak of World War 2 an increasing number were aware of the latest domestic fashions, were able to afford them, and (more importantly) considered it desirable to have a presentable home that reflected contemporary taste. All these factors would influence the design and contents of the prefabs of the 1940s. So home-centred was the contemporary British family that as the country prepared for war in 1939 the 'Britain by Mass Observation' project noted with concern that,

> the interest in oneself and one's own home has predominated far and away over international and general political concerns … an Englishman's home is still his castle.[17]

Despite the boom in suburban building, with almost 50 per cent more houses in 1941 than there had been in 1921, Britain still remained desperately short of housing. Increased employment in the late 1930s had led to a lower age of marriage and a need for more homes. Slums that should have been cleared in the 1920s survived, and many people were living in substandard accommodation. The new housing rarely catered for the lower classes as landowners and local councils controlled the housing types that were erected.

For those who could not afford the cost of a speculatively built home (around £500 for a three-bedroom semi in the late 1930s) there was always the option of self-build. Plots could be purchased for around £5, and several magazines catered for the growing number of people who travelled to their site at weekends and in holidays to build their 'dream homes'.

Despite these changes hundreds of thousands remained in inadequate accommodation. Squatting became increasingly common, even among the working population. By the outbreak of World War 2, Britain had a pressing need for housing, and many married couples had to share a home with their in-laws or rent rooms in damp and inadequate houses.

[1] See John Gloag and Derek Bridgewater, *A History of Cast Iron in Architecture*, Allen & Unwin 1948.
[2] See Kendall 1971.
[3] R B White reviews the various committees and changes in legislation affecting working-class housing in his *Prefabrication, A History of its Development in Great Britain*, HMSO 1965, pages 22–90.
[4] To paraphrase Prime Minister David Lloyd George.
[5] As reported in the *National Housing Manual* of 1923.
[6] R B White 1965 provides an excellent review of prefabrication between the wars.
[7] Architect Clough Williams-Ellis campaigned for a revival of these ancient building techniques through his *Cottage Building in Cob, Pisé, Chalk & Clay*, Country Life 1919; an enlarged third edition published in 1947 promoted the use of earth in the post-World War 2 housing programmes.
[8] An estate of Boot Houses on the Castelnau Estate in Barnes, London SW13, was still standing when visited in the early 1990s.
[9] Described in *Concrete and Constructional Engineering*, December 1923.
[10] Further information on these inter-war prefabricated concrete homes can be found in *Post-War Building Studies No. 1, House Construction*, HMSO 1944, pages 56–58.
[11] Further information on these 1930s timber prefabs can be found in *Post-War Building Studies No.1*, pages 67–71. See also *A Guide to Non-traditional Housing in Scotland*, Scottish Executive Building Division 2001.
[12] Statistics from Cox 1945, page 17.
[13] See Derek Kerr, *Railway Sleeper Buildings*, Scottish Vernacular Buildings Group 1986.
[14] See Andrew Saint, *Towards a Social Architecture, the Role of School Building in Post-War England*, Yale 1987, pages 1–35.
[15] Ravetz and Turkington, *The Place of Home. English Domestic Environments 1914–2000*, E & F N Spon 1995, page 20
[16] See Andrew Thorpe, *Britain in the 1930s*, Blackwell 1992.
[17] Madge C and T Harrison, *Britain by Mass Observation*, Penguin Books 1939, page 217.

After the last war we heard a good deal about homes for heroes, and we are now
hearing a good deal about the New Jerusalem which is to be built after this war. I do not
think that the country is likely to stand a second disappointment.[1]

The need for instant housing

When the air-raid sirens fell silent in March 1945 more than 3 million houses remained damaged; a quarter of all the homes in Britain. London had been badly hit by the V2 rocket attacks of 1944, when 84,000 homes were destroyed in acres of flames. In Birmingham a total of 71 air raids had destroyed 12,000 houses, and left another 25,000 without windows. By V-E Day (8 May 1945) there were 40,000 families needing homes on Birmingham's Housing Register alone, and it was a similar scenario in many other large towns and cities. Only seven of Clydebank's homes remained undamaged.

Around 200,000 new houses were built during the war, but the construction rate was almost a tenth of what it had been in the years before 1939. The problem was exacerbated by the fact that homes were not maintained during the war, and living conditions declined for many. People had to make do without glass in windows and live with tarpaulins on the roof. As early as 1942 Edwin Fairchild introduced his series of *Design for Britain* pamphlets, claiming that,

> There is no doubt that when the War is over the first task to which the Government
> of the day will have to commit itself will be that of an extensive building
> programme … Materials will be short, sea transport will have enormously

9/ Rebuilding the streets of Coventry in 1945. Bombing raids had destroyed the medieval city centre, and made tens of thousands homeless.

diminished, while that of rail and road will need overhauling. Labour too, will be short.

The end of the war saw a large number of newly married couples looking for a home for the families they had planned but postponed. There were half a million marriages every year during the war, with the majority of newlyweds sharing the houses of their in-laws. A larger number of women than usual were of child-bearing age, and a baby boom added pressure. Housing conditions became increasingly cramped as relatives from war-damaged homes doubled or trebled the occupancy of the houses that remained unscathed. And the situation was made worse by the fact that the population grew by a million during the war.

> My parents, my two sisters and I, all lived in a one-roomed bedsit in Liverpool, so one of my sisters and myself were sent to my grandparents in Maghull. As this meant the family were split up, my parents were put on an emergency housing list. At that time Liverpool council had several hutment sites on the outskirts of Liverpool which had been built in 1941 for refugees and army personnel, and decided to put families there whilst waiting for new houses to be completed.
> /June Sowerby

The government was particularly conscious of the immediate housing needs of ex-servicemen and evacuees, recalling the public anger at the failure to provide adequate accommodation for 'returning heroes' after World War 1. Servicemen not only required instant homes, they had high expectations about the standards of housing the government should provide. Surveys showed that

10/ Island Farm PoW camp 198 in Bridgend, South Wales. Typical of the concrete hutments erected across Britain for temporary military and civilian use, this example was used to hold some of the Third Reich's highest-ranking officers prior to their appearance at the Nuremberg war trials.

11/ 12/

people felt that their homes should contain the latest electric appliances, as well as an inside toilet and bathing facilities, and hot water on tap. These new developments were seen as the mark of modernity and an end to drudgery. The general willingness to 'make do' during the war years dissipated as people expected to see the new Britain for which they had been fighting. Building societies jumped on the bandwagon and produced booklets aimed at returning servicemen, such as one titled *That House in Civvy Street* published by the Abbey National in February 1945.

By the summer of 1946 thousands of people were squatting in disused wartime camps, and local authorities were forced to provide them with elec-

11/ Typical Nissen hut accommodation at Rackheath, Norwich in 1944. Note the laundry hanging out to dry and the careful maintenance of bicycles. 12/ Cutting grass by hand outside one of the Rackheath Nissens.

tricity and running water.[2] The London Communist Party even initiated a brief occupation of Kensington's most expensive properties.

Prefabrication as an answer
The housing crisis and the war itself encouraged the government to adopt an interventionist policy. Although there were large differences between the 1942 estimates of the number of new homes required (the Ministry of Health said 400,000 a year,[3] the Ministry of Works said 7 million in a decade[4]), it was clear that the traditional construction industry simply could not meet such a high output. The government looked to prefabrication as the answer to the immediate post-war housing crisis for complex reasons. Standardisation of new homes and their contents potentially meant huge savings through bulk buying that could be reflected in lower rents. Rivalry between the Ministries of Works and Health, increased enthusiasm for prefabrication among key government players, and the links between important industrialists and government all played a part.[5] And the prefabs were just as much about getting the women out of the factories to enable Beveridge to achieve his promised 'full employment'. If women could be encouraged to settle and start families by providing adequate accommodation for them, then men could take their jobs. Detached prefab bungalows that were rented only to families with young children were effectively a way of the government reinforcing traditional nuclear family values.

Government publicity in favour of prefabrication stressed that materials and skilled construction workers were in short supply, and the demand for housing was immediate and acute. One important consideration in favour of prefabs was the weight of the materials used in construction, and the costs of transportation and man-hours. A normal (brick-built) house of six rooms weighed about 125 tons and had about 53,000 separate parts,[6] yet early experimental aluminium prefabs weighed just 1.9 tons. Hundreds of thousands of permanent homes were planned (many of them using prefabricated parts), but prefabricated temporary bungalows would provide the 'quick fix' that Britain desperately needed.

Wartime prefab experiments
The government experimented with prefabricated housing during the war through the Ministry of Supply's hutment programme. Some, such as those at Malpas in Newport, were supplied as an empty shell with a combustion stove, and residents had to provide their own internal partitions. Simple semi-prefabricated huts proved ideal for temporary barracks and hostels to house essential workers in key locations around Britain. It was particularly convenient to use prefabricated huts that were easily demountable as work shifted from area to area. Various schemes included curved corrugated iron and asbestos sheets, sawdust concrete, plywood and plasterboard. The Ministry of Works Standard Hut had reinforced-concrete posts and roof beams, and brick, clay-block or wood-wool infilling.

Wartime employment manufacturing munitions and artillery familiarised the public with the principle of mass production and the idea that construction could be achieved quickly through using universal components. If military supplies could be constructed on a machine production line, then there was no reason why their temporary houses couldn't be manufactured in the same way. However, people's experiences in the temporary barracks, hutments and Nissen huts meant that they would automatically associate prefabricated housing

13/ 14/

with poor-quality, inadequate accommodation. It was important that any investigation into prefabrication must result in homes that looked different to wartime hutments and felt more solid and permanent than those short-life shacks.

By January 1943 a project to build single-storey houses at Kilmarnock experimented with wood-wool slabs for walls, and had a back-to-back prefab-

13/ Prototype for the Weir Paragon prefab bungalow erected in the summer of 1944 in Edinburgh. This system, devised by G & J Weir Ltd of Glasgow, was intended for post-war rural housing in Scotland, but was never part of the Temporary Housing Programme. 14/ Interior view of the Weir Paragon bungalow, showing the pressed steel sheet construction. 15/ page 32: Two-storey prefab prototype erected by Tarran Industries Ltd on 2 May 1944. Photograph taken at 8 am. 16/ page 33: Eight hours after construction began the Tarran home was complete.

ricated plumbing unit between the bathroom and kitchen. In June the Ministry of Works appointed a 'Controller of Experimental Building Development' who oversaw all applications for experimental work. In the first eight months private individuals and local authorities submitted some 559 proposals to the Controller. Eighty-seven of these suggestions for complete houses were carried forward for further development and consideration alongside the experiments carried out by the Ministry itself.[7]

In 1943 prefabricated cottages were erected in Brecon, Mid Wales. They were part of a programme of a thousand homes for key agricultural workers planned by the Ministry of Agriculture and supplied by the Ministry of Works. In the event less than a hundred of these concrete-section prefabs were constructed after Ministers were disappointed by the cramped accommodation that they provided.[8]

Tarran Industries of Hull was a private construction firm that had been enthusiastic about prefabrication since the mid 1930s. It was the contractor for the celebrated Quarry Hill flats of 1935, the largest prewar experiment in prefabrication. During the war Tarran supplied 9000 prefab timber huts to the War Department. By August 1943 Tarran was exhibiting the single-storey Mk III Tarran system at Conway Hall in London. It had walls of sawdust concrete and a flat roof covered with three layers of felt and bitumen. Mr Tarran announced to the press that he could produce 100,000 a year.[9] Less than a year later Tarran was demonstrating how it could construct attractive timber-framed two-storey concrete prefab homes in as little as eight hours![10]

17/ Cartoon by Emett from *Punch* magazine, commenting on the use of recycled aircraft aluminium in the production of the AIROH Aluminium Bungalow.

"*I say, that's awfully nice! I wonder what it WAS!*"

While the government was exhibiting its own prefab bungalow prototype in May 1944, Tarran was demonstrating his two-storey house. In an experiment designed to illustrate that unskilled community groups could build their own prefab homes, just like the tradition in Sweden, it took eight men and four women just eight hours to erect the house. It had factory-made plumbing units on both floors and was given a choice of stone finishes.[11] The BBC picked up on Tarran's publicity and produced a radio programme for the Home Service entitled *Building a Cottage in One Hour*.[12] These independent efforts won Tarran a place in the wartime Temporary Housing Programme (THP).

Another manufacturer that received contracts under the THP through a genuine interest in prefabrication was Uni-Seco. The Seco system could be used to produce both single- and two-storey prefab houses of cement sheets on timber frames, and in a variety of unit arrangements. Other wartime British experiments include prefabs by the City Architect of Coventry, D E E Gibson (two-storeys on a steel frame) and the City Engineer of Birmingham (steel frame and asbestos cladding, but intended for brick cladding after the war). Unibuilt houses with flat concrete roofs erected near Coventry also attracted the attention of the architectural press.

In Penilee, Scotland, Glasgow Corporation was constructing factory-made reinforced foam-slag concrete panel homes which boasted better insulation than standard 11-inch cavity brick walls. Also manufactured in Glasgow were the steel-clad Weir Paragon bungalows that were erected at Sighthill in Edinburgh in summer 1944.[13] These were intended for rural housing in Scotland after the war. The Braithwaite Unit Construction system erected asbestos-clad prefabs with concrete roofs on the London County Council's Watling estate, while Jicwood bungalows were the first to use stressed-skin plywood panels.

This idea was directly inspired by American prefabs, and it enabled the bungalows to be erected with each wall in one piece, and the floor and roof each in two pieces.

British Iron & Steel Federation houses built at the Government Experimental Housing Site at Northolt, Middlesex, were erected in various claddings, and would form the prototypes of the post-war permanent prefabs now referred to as BISFs. Also at Northolt, the Ministry of Works experimented with two-storey blocks of flats which they estimated could be built with about half the usual site labour. As with so many of these wartime experiments, the prefabs were steel-framed and faced with precast-concrete slabs. While all these manufacturers were experimenting in prefabrication in construction, others, such as Denham, were concentrating on the prefabrication of 'Mechanical Cores' for prefab homes. These had either back-to-back plumbing units for bathrooms and kitchens, or vertical versions for two-storey homes.

The Temporary Housing Programme

> 'Prefabrication' is a word on everyone's lips nowadays and, as is always the case with the fashionable word of the moment, it is often used very loosely. Does it really mean anything? Is it the new-found panacea for all our building problems, or is it a stunt or meaningless catchword?[14]

The start of the post-war prefab programme can be traced to 1942, when it appeared that the immediate threat of invasion had passed and people's interest turned to the reconstruction of their bombed homes. It was recognised even at this point that Britain would have to construct some 3 to 4 million new

18/

homes in the decade after the war, and the pressure on the government to provide for the people was acute. The issue of housing was first raised in the King's Speech to Parliament of 11 November 1942, and from then on was a subject of much discussion.

During a debate on housing in May 1943 the government decided to invest in a prototype temporary steel bungalow. Following an announcement about the prototype by Lord Portal, Minister of Works, on 8 February 1944, the prototype became known as the *Portal* bungalow.[15] The architects were Mr C J Mole (for the Ministry of Works) and Mr A W Kenyon (consulting architect). Not a truly machine-made house, the bungalow was constructed by hand by the motor manufacturer Briggs Motor Bodies of Dagenham and the Pressed Steel Company of Cowley.

On 26 March 1944 Prime Minister Winston Churchill announced the much-publicised Ministry of Works Emergency Factory-made House Programme:

19/   20/

> The swift production of these temporary houses is the only way in which the immediate needs of our people can be met in the four or five years that follow the war.

The 'temporary' label was part of the effort to persuade people to accept interim housing of lightweight construction; the government was careful to illustrate that the temporary prefabs were only one form of factory-produced

18/ The prototype steel Portal bungalow exhibited in Edinburgh in June 1944. In May it had been displayed at the Tate Gallery in London. The lobby entrance arrangement differed from that on the production model. **19/** Two ATS auxiliaries inspecting the kitchen of the prefab home they were told they could expect after the war. **20/** Lance Corporal D Small of Gateshead seated at a Utility dressing table in the steel Portal bungalow displayed in Edinburgh.

housing. The label also acted as an assurance to the building trade unions that feared the loss of jobs. The building trade was greatly reduced during wartime (down from a million workers in 1939 to less than 400,000 in the war), and factory-made houses required few skills in their final construction. Labelling the programme as temporary was also intended to soften any hard feelings created by the fact that central government was overriding the autonomy of local government – unusually, the programme was financed by the state rather than the local authority. [16]

By May 1944 the first prototype was ready for public exhibition at the Tate Gallery in London; it then moved to Edinburgh in June. Beveridge had suggested that the war was going to change society, and the radically modern prefab design that met the eyes of the invited Press appeared as firm evidence that there was now a new way of thinking. The very fact that people were being invited to debate the prefab design and make constructive comments for alterations and improvements was a departure for the government. Military personnel were invited to view the Portal, and one was even erected next to the pyramids of Giza for the inspection of the British armed forces in Egypt. [17]

The bungalow was radically different from traditional municipal housing, such as the council estates built after World War 1 which adopted Georgian-style sash windows in a look popularised by Louis de Soissons at Welwyn Garden City. In contrast, this single-storey shallow-roofed rectangular home offered a reminder of the flat-roofed Hollywood villas that millions would have seen on their weekly visits to picture houses. It represented perhaps the first real impact of Modern Movement architecture on mass housing in Britain.

The press identified Churchill with this prefab prototype, dubbing it the 'Churchill Steel House'.[18] Much mirth resulted from the news that a car factory had manufactured the bungalow, people asking why it didn't have windscreen wipers fitted to the windows. The contents, however, appear to have impressed visitors to the Tate. The level of fixtures, fittings and equipment was far beyond what people would have expected: the prototype had a cooker, sink and refrigerator built into steel fitted units, a full-size bath and space for a combined clothes-washing boiler. Few of the people who were eligible for the prefab homes would have enjoyed these mod cons before, and the fitted refrigerator was a particular talking point. Hot air from the living room fire was ducted to warm the bedrooms, and there were fitted units and cupboards carefully designed into the internal walls. People would rarely have seen so many fitted cupboards in a home, and (considering the furniture shortage) were sure to welcome them.

The Portal provided two bedrooms, a kitchen, living room and bathroom with an overall living space of 616 square feet (57 square metres). Each of the bedrooms was an acceptable 125 square feet (11.6 square metres), and the living room 145 square feet (13.5 square metres). There was even room for a separate toilet and shed (this being housed in the flat-roofed extension near the entrance). In design terms the back-to-back plumbing 'heart unit' of the kitchen and bathroom was novel (probably inspired by US examples), and the house was unusual in that there was minimal circulation space; rooms opened off each other rather than off a central hallway.

The estimated cost per bungalow was £550 at the time it was first exhibited outside the tate Gallery in May 1944, making it slightly more expensive than a traditionally constructed brick house at £510. Lord Portal reminded those who frowned on this fact that:

> … the whole object of erecting these emergency houses is to make a substantial contribution to the interregnum period, using as little site labour as possible, to enable our labour force to build itself up for the permanent building programme.[19]

Some, such as Liverpool City Architect L H Keay, agreed, stating that although he hated the Portal design, prefabs were a necessary evil until the construction trade was back on its feet.[20] Keay went on to design his own prototype prefab in Liverpool, as did the Housing Director of Leeds, but neither was accepted by London, and none was authorised under the Temporary Housing Programme.[21] There was evidently some friction between the local authorities and the Ministry of Health, as the councils perceived that central government was meddling in housing, which was their responsibility. The municipal housing of the 1930s had been of a lower standard than in the 1920s (reflecting the assertion that council housing was suitable only for ex-slum dwellers).[22] By fitting a quality wash boiler, fridge and cooker in the prefabs, the state was effectively setting a precedent for new levels of equipment in housing, and local authorities would now have to provide similar facilities. The luxury fittings of the prefab implied that they were intended for a better class of people, and thus they could be considered as tools for social change.

Not everyone agreed that the temporary prefabs were necessary, arguing that they were a waste of time and resources. The majority of critics claimed that the available funds should be put into constructing permanent homes. Others referred to the Portal as 'Heartbreak House' (George Bernard Shaw) and 'The Damn Tin Can',[23] complaining that with just two bedrooms the bungalows would be too small for the average family. Others made more constructive criticism: Walter Segal suggested that the Portals should be erected opposite proposed permanent housing sites, so that communities could remain together when the time came to move 'across the road'.[24] Praise came from some unexpected quarters. M H Baillie-Scott, the eminent Arts and Crafts architect (who was not noted for his love of modern contemporary architecture), declared that he would be content in a prefab if he survived the war.[25]

Following the comments on the May 1944 prototype the Portal bungalow was revised. The shed was removed from the shell of the building, providing increased storage and an enlarged hall. The ceiling was raised in height (to $7\frac{1}{2}$ feet, 2.3 metres), a door was added from the kitchen into the garden, and another from the hallway directly into the living room. A revised Portal was exhibited in the autumn of 1944 alongside three other temporary house prototypes – the Arcon, Uni-Seco and Tarran prefabs. Early in 1945 the Spooner bungalow was on exhibition at the Tate Gallery.

In October 1944 a Housing Act authorised £150 million for the Temporary Housing Programme, to provide 250,000 homes. However, within a few weeks it became apparent that the steel (Portal) bungalow was not viable as the output of the steel industry was still required for the war effort. The programme shifted to concentrate on temporary homes that were only partly prefabricated, with the main assembly occurring on-site. The Arcons, Uni-Secos and Tarrans were all framed structures that had prefab panels bolted on during erection, so were ideal. The steel Portal was eventually abandoned in favour of a model which took advantage of the surplus capacity in aluminium production. The Aircraft Industries Research Organisation for Housing (AIROH) developed the Aluminium Bungalow to fit the bill. With an appearance similar to that of the Portal, this prefab was the last to be exhibited for public scrutiny, in the summer of 1945.[26]

 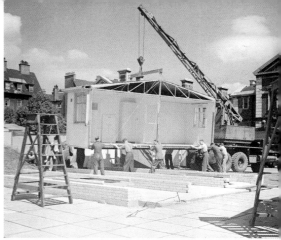

21/ 22/

In July 1945 the British people rejected the politics of conservatism; Clement Attlee won the general election with a surprise landslide victory. The Labour Party had fought the election with a promise of 5 million new homes. By the time the new government took office it was clear that the cost of individual prefabs was considerably higher than had been anticipated. The most expensive (the Aluminium Bungalow) was now £1365; considerably more than traditionally constructed homes. The new Labour government addressed the housing shortage with the 1946 Housing Act that guaranteed subsidies and

21/ The four sections of the AIROH Aluminium Bungalow arrive at the Tate Gallery for public display on 22 June 1945. 22/ The first of the four sections is craned into place. Note the fitted kitchen cupboard, which is also constructed of aluminium alloy. 23/ The final section is pushed into place. After welding the seams the house was ready for inspection.

23/

grants for new houses, and a national annual homebuilding target of 240,000 new houses was announced.

Promoting prefabrication

> With the prospect of a not too distant termination of the war, prefabrication has become a question of major interest and importance. Hardly a week passes but some project or experiment is reported in the technical press.[27]

The government knew that it would take considerable work to persuade the British public that the radical and innovative prefabs were suitable accommodation. It was for this reason that public discussion was invited on the Tate prototypes, and the BBC broadcast programmes analysing the virtues of prefabrication. The publicity developed a life of its own and popular discussion of the Temporary Housing Programme was seen across the board, from high-brow architectural debates down to the cartoons in *Punch* and other magazines and newspapers.

The end of the war saw a flurry of publications aimed at architects and the general public, all of them espousing the virtues of prefabrication in answering the housing crisis. A major influence on the progress of prefabrication in the UK was the publication of a large survey which had been begun by members of the staff of the Directorate of Post-War Building of the Ministry of Works back in 1943. The aim had been to assess the scope and range of prefabrication in countries such as Germany, France, the USA, and elsewhere. In particular, America had never broken with the timber housing tradition and, along with Sweden, was the object of much interest. Architect Walter Gropius

was consulted on his copper prefab homes, and Konrad Wachsmann of the General Panel Corporation in New York was asked to provide information on his prefabs.

The Ministry of Works published the results of their 'Survey of Prefabrication' in 1945,[28] a large document by D Dex Harrison that was then the most extensive and carefully researched comparative study of prefabrication undertaken anywhere in the world. The document was distributed to government departments, local authorities, and individual architects and opinion formers. It included the details of every known prefab manufacturer in the world, and an impressive 51 British companies/systems and architects, all working on prefab-

24/ Ada Ellis was bombed out of her house in London's East End in 1939, and qualified for this Uni-Seco prefab in 1945. She was told it was only temporary (five years), but lived there until it was demolished in 1970.

rication by 1945. These included Boulton & Paul, Frederick Gibberd, Ministry of Works huts, Orlit and F R S Yorke. The study concluded that the best prefabricated systems were composite, and not the 'all-concrete', 'all-timber' or 'all-steel' prefab home.

Britain had been aware of the huge Swedish timber prefab estates before World War 2,[29] but the end of the war saw the publication of several popular studies of the Swedish and American prefab types. In Sweden timber prefabs had been produced on a very large scale for so long that they were the regarded as traditional. Architect Bernard Cox published a 36-page pamphlet, *Prefabricated Homes*, in June 1945; the cover drawing was by his well-known colleague Ernö Goldfinger. So great was the interest among the public that the first impression sold out in a couple of weeks. The pamphlet featured British, Swedish and American prefabs and prototypes, including the radical US 'Bubble House' which was formed by pumping concrete over an inflated canvas bag and cutting out the windows and doors. The resulting igloo-shaped homes were then given incongruous neo-Georgian sash windows.

The celebrated architect Hugh Casson published *Homes by the Million. An account of housing methods of the USA 1940–1945* with Penguin, thus ensuring a popular market at just 2s 6d.

> America needed houses and got them. If, backed by their experience, we can show the same initiative and energy, then we can get them, too.[30]

Lavishly illustrated, the book promoted the replication of the US model in the reconstruction of Europe. Particular emphasis was given to describing the temporary prefabricated homes constructed by the Tennessee Valley Authority

(TVA) where 10,000 homes were delivered on the back of trailers, often in just two pieces. The well-publicised TVA prefabs that could be constructed in less than a day found their way into virtually all the published British texts on the virtues of prefabrication. The use of power tools such as electric drills increased the high output per man-hour of the American technician. Casson concluded that post-war housing must be the responsibility of the state, that the construction industry must be reorganised to increase prefabrication production, and that the new houses must be accompanied by communal facilities.

25/ The Tennessee Valley Authority Trailer Home, designed in 1939, influenced British prefab design. 26/ page 50: The two sections of the TVA prefab being winched together. These remarkable photographs were featured widely in British publications. 27/ page 51: An estate of TVAs. The US government could move these fully mobile prefabs from town to town as the need for accommodation arose.

26/

50/

In December of 1945, *Houses: Permanence and Prefabrication* proposed prefabrication as a solution to Britain's 4-million-homes shortage. It pointed out that factory production was ideal in Britain's unpredictable climate, and that it was only 'the fear and ignorance of obstructive and sectional interests' that prevented us moving forward into a major prefabrication project.[31] The following month Aneurin Bevan (then at the Ministry of Health) wrote the foreword to *Homes for the People*,[32] claiming that the new homes that were needed could be provided in this 'age of invention' by new thinking in house construction. The book went on to recommend nationalisation of all the land in the UK, and the revision of bye-laws that restricted innovative construction materials and techniques. John Gloag and Grey Wornum's 1946 *House Out of Factory* mixed photographs from America with the THP Arcons and numerous permanent British prefab types. Other titles, such as Howard Robertson's 1947 *Reconstruction and the Home* concentrated on interiors, and how fitted units saved time and space.

---

[1] Official Report from the House of Commons, 4 May 1943, Vol 389, col. 81–82.
[2] Robins 2001, page 12, described how Malpas Court Military Camp was officially renamed 'Malpas Communal Housing Camp' when squatters moved in.
[3] Health 1942.
[4] Works 1942.
[5] For an in-depth exploration of the administrative process which led up to the THP see Gay 1986 (also summarised in Gay 1987).
[6] Statistics provided by H V Boughton in *Building*, October 1943.
[7] Statistics provided in Cox 1945.
[8] Discussed further in Kohan 1952, page 377.
[9] Quoted in Neel 1943, page 212.
[10] See *The Architects' Journal*, 27 July 1944.
[11] 'Tarran revised system of construction', page 154 in *Architectural Design & Construction*, July 1944.

[12] As reported in *The Architect and Building News*, 2 June 1944, pages 131–132.
[13] *The Architect and Building News*, 1 September 1944.
[14] Bernard Cox introducing his 1945 booklet *Prefabricated Homes*. The first print run sold out in less than a month.
[15] Lord Portal also gave his name to the construction term 'Portal frame' which is still in use today.
[16] Suggested by Vale 1990, page 110.
[17] Reported in the reader's letters of *Picture Post*, 23 June 1945.
[18] See 'The Churchill Steel House' in *Building*, Vol. 19 (1944), page 122.
[19] Official Report of the House of Lords, 1943–44, Vol. 131, col. 565.
[20] BBC 1944, page 35.
[21] Keay received permission to erect a quantity of his bungalows in Liverpool, but it is unclear whether R A H Livett's prefabs (with bay windows) in Leeds ever went into production.
[22] Gay 1987, page 408.
[23] *Building*, May 1944, page 141.
[24] *The Architect and Building News*, 8 September 1944, page 152.
[25] 'The MOW Emergency House', *The Builder*, 4 August 1944, page 141.
[26] Works 1948, page 2.
[27] Cox 1945, page 18.
[28] See D Harrison *et al* 1945.
[29] Described in the *RIBA Journal* in August 1939, in Denby 1938 and in *The Architects' Journal* on 7 March 1935.
[30] Casson 1946, page 148.
[31] Quote from the dustjacket of Anthony 1945. Note that Hugh Anthony, the 'author' was 'a pseudonym which conceals the names of two well-known young architects'.
[32] Association of Building Technicians 1946.

28/ The Aluminium Bungalow was the first British house to be entirely prefabricated on a production line. This example from an estate near Stroud was occupied for half a century before it was demolished in 1997.

the temporary housing programme/

> … we shall improve human beings. We shall improve them by teaching them, by legislation, by planning for them a better environment and a saner world. We are going to build a new Britain after the war.[1]

Thirteen different prefab types were erected under the 1944 Temporary Housing Programme, all of them following a standard two-bedroom format as prescribed by the Portal prototype. All but the imported US models used a standard Ministry of Works 'heart' unit of back-to-back kitchen and bathroom plumbing.

Prefabs with a floor area of just 635 square feet (59 square metres) were built across Britain wherever housing needs were greatest. Occasionally just a handful of bungalows would replace bomb-damaged homes, and would be inserted into otherwise traditional street façades. In other areas, estates of hundreds of prefabs were built on brown- and greenfield sites. Few counties didn't have prefabs allocated to them, and it is no surprise that the towns that had suffered the most during the war received the greatest number of temporary homes. Coventry, Liverpool, Southampton, Portsmouth, Manchester, Bristol, Cardiff, Newport, Plymouth, Birmingham, Belfast, Hull, Clydeside, Bath, Norwich, York and Canterbury all had prefab estates. More than 10,000 prefabs were erected in Greater London alone, in all manner of neighbourhoods including prestigious Blackheath.[2] There were soon queues of people at council housing offices demanding they be considered for a prefab.

> Mother went to the housing office every Wednesday and my father went every Saturday to see where they were on the list. Such was the demand that the housing officer had a nervous breakdown. In the end my mother found a councillor that she vaguely knew, contacted him and they got a prefab. /Mary Sprakes

The prefabs were allocated according to need, and it was rare for anyone without a child to be allocated one. Those that were often had special medical requirements, such as TB that had been exacerbated by living in damp rented accommodation. Having two children improved your chances, and some people timed their second child in order to improve their position on the housing list. Once in the prefab, tenants were limited to a maximum of six children under ten years of age, although few had more than two. A few estates were erected exclusively for key workers, such as one for the Birmingham City Police Force at Edgbaston.

Often German and Italian prisoners of war undertook the construction work which took between a few hours and a few days per bungalow. Several cases are recorded of PoWs crafting toys for the prefab children, and this usually brought them bowls of food from grateful mothers.

> When we had the keys to move in there were no pavements laid, or entrance down to the house. Every day, German PoWs came by lorry to work on the estate. Seeing our predicament, they very kindly laid a few blocks as stepping stones for us to get to the door 'mud free'. Seeing we weren't really allowed to fraternise, when I was baking there would always be some small warm cakes, left on the doorstep, for them as a thank you. /Ruth Haynes recalling her Aluminium Bungalow at Honicknowle, Plymouth

Doris Bendall who lived in a Bristol prefab, even invited a couple in for

29/ Elevations of the Aluminium Bungalow, designed by the Aircraft Industries Research Organisation on Housing.

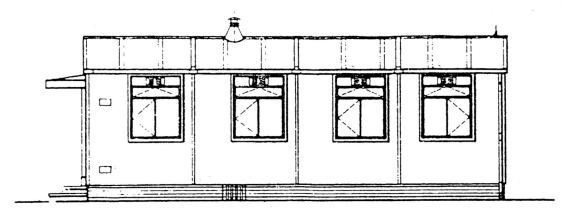

BACK ELEVATION

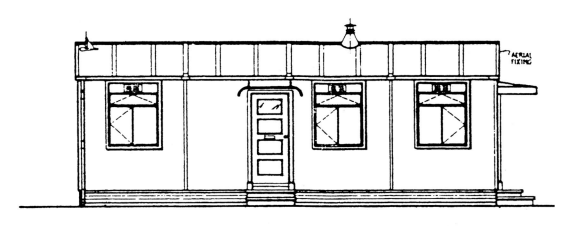

FRONT ELEVATION

Christmas dinner: 'They carved a toy horse for the children before they came, and they were very polite.'

Some towns had large estates made up of just one prefab type – in Newport in South Wales 671 of the 750 prefabs built were Mk V Arcons.[3] Other places, such as Bristol, erected different types in different suburbs, leaving them with a rich prefab heritage. It doesn't follow that houses were distributed in the areas close to their manufacture. Hull, for example, was the home of both Tarran Industries and Spooner Ltd, but estates of Aluminium Bungalows (constructed in the west of England) were still erected there. The US prefab system, where temporary 'factories' would be erected on the building site, was not adopted; instead selected manufacturers brought in components

30/ Aluminium Bungalow estate at Folkestone, 1949. Note how there are no roads between the houses, just footpaths. Few of the residents would have had cars.

from across the country, and then redistributed the prefabs as individually prepared packages.

Considering their short projected life it is interesting to note the considerable thought that often went into the layout of prefab estates. Although some authorities built them in monotonous rows that highlighted their 'cookie-cutter' uniformity, many councils introduced the estate layouts that they intended to use when replacing the temporary accommodation a decade later. Several estates were arranged following the formal geometry then popular for council estates – with large greens, crescents and a generally thoughtful layout. The Shrublands estate of 711 Arcons in Great Yarmouth radiated out from a circular hub, and the Pleasant View estate of Aluminium Bungalows in Southampton had what residents referred to as the 'big green' and the 'little green'. Such planning contributed to the instant sense of community that many felt upon moving into their temporary homes.

Prefabs had to meet a range of criteria. They had to:

1. last for at least ten years (US imported) or 15 years (UK types)
2. make best use of the materials that were in abundant supply
3. make minimal use of timber, even for garden fencing
4. avoid the use of bricks, even for chimneys
5. use the government-approved 'heart unit' of back-to-back kitchen and bathroom plumbing (UK types)
6. use parts that were as far as possible factory-made
7. use ex-factory units with dimensions that meant they were easily transportable by road (i.e. with a maximum width of $7^1/_2$ feet)
8. be able to be easily and quickly constructed on site, making minimal use of traditional skills.

Despite their short life expectancy, prefabs benefited from remarkably advanced planning and design. All shared a common layout with two bedrooms, a living room, bathroom and kitchen, a large garden and shed (often an Anderson air-raid shelter with a bricked-up rear wall and door to the front). Some included the toilet in the bathroom, but most retained it in a separate room. For most of the original occupants the prefab would be their first experience of living on a single storey, with an inside toilet and bathroom. Not many of the original residents would have enjoyed the luxury of living in a detached home before, and fewer still would have had such a large garden. The prefab bungalow prioritised middle-class living, having all mod-cons, a large garden, and a tradesman's entrance from the garden straight into the kitchen, creating an image of privacy that residents had probably not previously experienced in terraced urban homes. It has been argued that the interwar generation was the most family-minded and home-centred one in history,[4] and certainly the physical isolation on all four sides gave the prefabs maximum 'individual identity'.

The most popular architectural style between the wars had invoked the country-cottage look. Many of the prefab types provided a pared-down cottage image, with a central doorway flanked by a window on either side – just like the classic country cottage. Even the Mk II prototype had roses pinned to a pergola around the door. In the same way that 1930s semis had mixed the modern and traditional in a Moderne pastiche,[5] prefabs blended a simplified

31/ Plan of the Pleasant View estate of Aluminium Bungalows built on the outskirts of Southampton. Note the careful layout and planning with green areas for recreation and large garden plots. The houses on Canterbury and Swanmore Avenues are of standard construction.

country-cottage image with 'modernist' flat roofs and corner windows. The prefab was the best of both worlds for many residents – a detached cottage with a large garden and the latest labour-saving kitchen inside. Corner windows (on Uni-Secos and Tarrans) were themselves a reference to the new way of building as the corners were no longer structurally essential to the building as a whole. These, and the large metal-framed windows on Arcons, would have provided reminders of 1930s modernist architecture. Residents associated large windows with the large and bright interiors of modern architecture, and a new way of living. Even today, residents of the remaining Arcon bungalows say that the large picture windows are one of the main reasons why they would never move.

In the 1930s local authorities, building societies, and much of the public had rejected the hard-line modernist style that can be seen particularly in the Uni-Seco and US-imported prefabs with their virtually flat roofs. By the mid 1940s such sensibilities had to be swept away in the drive to construct affordable housing in the shortest possible time.

Aluminium Bungalow

The Aluminium Bungalow (B2) as developed by the Aircraft Industries Research Organisation for Housing (AIROH) was the first British home to be wholly manufactured and constructed on a production line.[6] As such it represented the epitome of the post-war prefab movement. Arriving from the factory in just four pieces, the Aluminium Bungalow (or AIROH, as it became known) could be bolted together on to a concrete or brick plinth in less than 24 hours, or 30–40 man-hours.[7] All fittings and paint finishes were added prior to delivery. It was the B2 that people refer to when they recall seeing prefab

house sections arriving on the back of lorries, and people moving in 'by tea time'. Similarly it is the Aluminium Bungalow to which we can trace the idea that war-damaged aircraft were literally melted down and recast as housing. It was, therefore, a powerful symbol of reconstruction.

The Aluminium Bungalow was the solution of the aluminium industry to the steel shortage that sounded the death knell for the steel-clad Portal design. A prototype was built by the Bristol Aeroplane Co., and exhibited behind Selfridge's department store in London in the summer of 1945 as part of the 'Aluminium from War to Peace Exhibition'. Jim Payne, a design engineer with the Ministry of Defence, used his experience designing the Mulberry Harbour

32/ **Ness Edwards MP (left) and local dignitaries at the opening of the Hendre estate of Aluminium Bungalows near Cardiff in June 1948. Most of the residents worked at the Nantgarw colliery.**

33/ Nadia Edwards standing outside her Aluminium Bungalow on the Sandfields estate in Port Talbot: 'It was fabulous, it was just like living in an outsized caravan.'

(a floating metal dock used in World War 2) to help hone the B2 design. In general the AIROH B2 was closer to the Portal in outward appearance than any of the other prefabs supplied through the THP. The fact that aircraft engineers had designed it also led to high standards of craftsmanship for interior details. What it didn't share with aircraft was their sleek aerodynamic design; considering the skilled designers that prepared the B2 design, its external appearance was not particularly exciting.

Being fully prefabricated, the houses would arrive ready on site with all interior fittings, appliances and final decorations. The important 'heart unit' came safely in one section. The services were carefully planned so that only one joint was needed for each of water, electricity, gas and sewage. This high level of prefabrication did have some negative consequences. As each of the four modules had to be a regular size for transportation purposes (7 1/2 feet wide by 22 1/2 feet long), the room dimensions all had to be either single- or double-lorry width. Thus the toilet ended up squashed into the bathroom, and the kitchen was not large.

The prefab itself was formed from extruded aluminium alloy sections, with a traditional pine floor. Most of the construction was in fact done by hand in the factory. Aerated concrete provided the (minimal) insulation to the wall panels, which were finished with plasterboard to the inside. Internal walls were insulated in a similar fashion. Window frames were also aluminium, as were the rainwater goods. Only the doors and door frames escaped being aluminium-made, and were of traditional timber construction. The final craning into position of the B2s made impressive viewing, and was featured in many newspapers.

Because they used some imported aluminium, AIROHs were expensive

35/

and wasteful, but the Ministry of Aircraft Production (under pressure from its client industries) secured their place in the THP programme. This fact has caused some to speculate that the THP was in fact more of a solution to the problem of how to engage the massively enlarged aluminium and steel industries after the war, and less an answer to the scarcity of traditional materials and shortage of construction skills.[8] Prefabricated homes were an ideal peacetime

34/ 22 Sunny Hill, Stroud, photographed shortly before demolition in 1996.
35/ 25 Sunny Hill, Stroud. Although this estate of Aluminium Bungalows was erected in 1948, the houses were not part of the official THP statistics, and were categorised as permanent homes.

product for the factories engaged in the war effort, as they transferred the skills involved in house construction into the factory. Homes could then be constructed across Britain using mostly unskilled labour.

Fifty-four thousand AIROH bungalows were constructed as part of the THP, despite being the most expensive of the popular types. Although the original AIROHs outlasted their intended life, in general they have not proved as hardy as those that were clad in asbestos-cement sheets (Arcon, Phoenix, etc.). From the start it was claimed that the bungalows could survive 'for at least forty years',[9] and indeed many did survive into the 1990s in remarkably original condition at Cam in Gloucestershire. Today only one AIROH B2 exists in original condition, and this has been moved to the Museum of Welsh Life near Cardiff, where it has been restored with a period interior.

Arcon Mk V

The Arcon was in many ways the most successful of the prefab types erected under the Temporary Housing Programme. At an estimated £1085 per unit, the Arcon was of average price, but being constructed of asbestos cement panels bolted on to a steel frame, it provided surprisingly long-lasting accommodation. With a stylised country-cottage appearance and sturdy construction, the Arcon generally outlived the other three main prefab types (Tarrans, Uni-Secos, and Aluminium Bungalows).

The Arcon group came together in April 1943 to design asbestos-clad demountable prefabs. The group included the architects Edric Neel, Raglan Squire, Rodney Thomas and Jim Gear, industrialists, and the construction firm Taylor Woodrow. (The Arcon name was derived from the phrase Architectural Consultants.)[10] The group started designing components from scratch, including the 'heart' plumbing unit. Like the model developed by the Ministry of Works, this was based on American designs. It differed, however, in incorporating the WC. In the end the Ministry of Works unit was exhibited (in spring 1944) before the Arcon design was complete, and the Arcon units were never put into production.

The Arcon Mk II was exhibited in spring 1944. It provided two-bedroom accommodation in a steel-framed structure clad in asbestos cement and lined internally with plasterboard. The structure was raised off the ground by small concrete piles that appeared to have been moulded from upturned flowerpots. The inspection date by Lord Portal fell in the middle of rocket attacks, and the staff recall painting the roof of the Arcon as a bomb fell on St Thomas's Hospital, just 300 yards down the Thames:

> There was no time to reach the ground and the safety of our blast wall, so we dropped flat on the asbestos cement we had just painted. In spite of all, the house was ready for the Minister's inspection. The small garden, laid overnight to give some relief from the harsh concrete of the site, glistened with recent watering. The roses, precariously pinned to the pergola, competed with the more pungent odour of the new paint.[11]

The Mk V Arcon differed from Aluminium Bungalows, Tarrans and Uni-Secos in the location of its hallway, which ran between the toilet and bedroom two rather than between the living room and bedroom one. Clever planning included an airing cupboard, drop-down kitchen table, fitted cupboards between the living room and main bedroom, and a fitted kitchen larder which was ventilated directly to the outside. Most were provided with an unused

36/   37/

Anderson shelter as storage for bicycles and tools. In practice most of these were used for storing coal.

Inside the Arcon the heating was provided by a central boiler, with hot air ducted through to the bedrooms, an idea that was probably inspired by American temporary housing, and one that apparently was never particularly effective. The windows were larger than any previously seen in small mass-market housing. The Mk II had a large weather canopy over the main entrance, reminiscent of a caravan awning, with a small area of decking below. The toilet was integrated with the main wall of plumbing. As the plumbing and general plan did not conform to the generic Portal plan Arcon was asked to revise the design. After various revisions the Mk III was designed (never built) and by September of 1944 the Mk IV (with separate toilet) was ready for exhibition at the Tate Gallery. Ministers and representatives from local authorities agreed that they were satisfied with the design, and Taylor Woodrow was asked to

38/

begin the production of 86,000 Arcon bungalows.[12] By the time the houses came to production the Mk IV had been fine-tuned into the Mk V, after each of the 390 separate components and sub-assemblies were rechecked for compatibility. The canopy had gone and the steel used for the frame had been changed for tubular section metal as supplies were still low. Remarkably, the

36/ An estate of Arcons at Newport, South Wales, each carefully positioned to gain maximum benefit of a south-facing slope. 37/ One of the 600 Arcon Mk V prefabs that were still in use in Newport, half a century after they were erected. 38/ An estate illustrating three prefab types at New Addington, Croydon. Arcons fill the foreground, Aluminium Bungalows are visible to the left of the background, and behind these stand two-storey BISF prefabs. 39/ pages 72–73: The Arcon Mk V was constructed using 390 components. Some of these are displayed here in a photograph taken at the Temporary Housing Distribution Centre, Liverpool, in 1946.

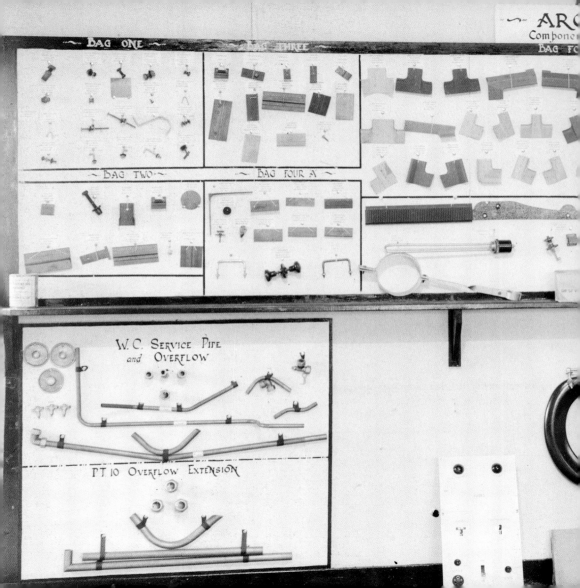

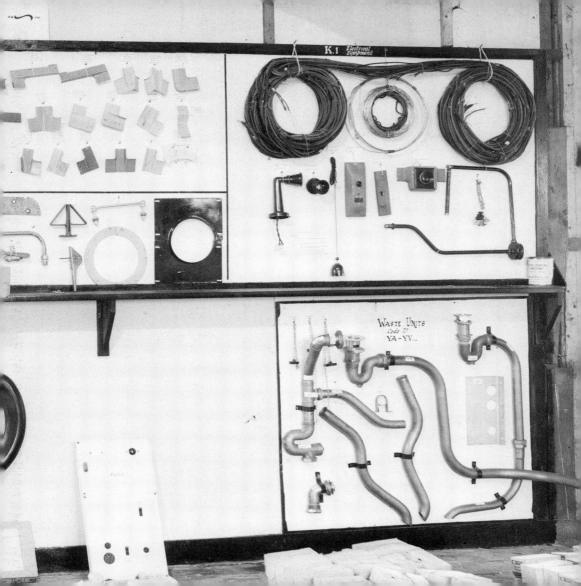

40/

41/

40/ One of a dozen or so Arcons exported to Ahmadi in Kuwait for employees of an oil company. Note the fly screens on the windows. Every morning a truck called the 'Bug Bomb' would pass and spray the prefabs with DDT to keep the insects down. 41/ Rhys John measuring the distance from his Arcon to the camera in order to get the picture in focus, 1953. Note the vents to the right of the door that provided fresh air to the larder cupboard behind. 42/ No. 46, Bishpool, Newport. Residents who bought their Arcons from the local council in the 1980s and 1990s were free to paint them in any colour they liked.

42/

whole process from exhibition of prototype to the time that the first family moved into a Mk V Arcon in July 1945 took only one year. Considering that the components were specially designed, and that all had to be redesigned at least once during the development of the final house, it was an impressive feat of design and engineering.

The Mk V Arcon was a successful collaboration between many manufacturers. Corby provided the steel, Darlington Rolling Mills the windows, and the asbestos sheeting came from Turners. Factories across England, Scotland and Wales produced components which were then collected in London prior to redistribution. The beauty of the Arcon was to be found in the design and forethought that went into the structure and the fixtures. Steel architraves, picture rails and skirting were all provided, which doubled up as novel ducting for the electric wiring. This enabled the switches and sockets to be fitted on to the architraves and skirting and no exposed wires were seen anywhere. Instead of a pointed ridge on the roof, a curved crown was provided, giving the building its characteristic appearance, and eliminating the need for steel supports at the apex. The roof was single-skin cement sheet, but the walls were double for extra strength. Internally, the panels walls were filled with glass-fibre quilt for insulation, the performance of which was claimed to equal that of a standard 11-inch cavity brick wall.

Finally, at total of 39,000 Arcon Mk Vs were erected under the THP, but the company went on to design permanent prefab houses and schools. These were never actually produced due to shortages of timber, hardboard and plywood, which made the project economically unviable. Unlike some of its contemporaries, the Arcon was designed to be demountable, and thus a use was anticipated for these humble bungalows after the initial 10–15-year lifespan under the THP. Several hundred Arcons remain in virtually original condition in Newport, South Wales at the time of writing.[13] Taylor Woodrow, the original building contractor, has sponsored the removal of a surviving Birmingham example for reconstruction at the Avoncroft Museum of Buildings at Bromsgrove.

43/ Despite being manufactured on a production line, the Arcon represented a romantic country cottage to some residents. This example stood at Hornchurch in Essex. 44/ pages 78–79: Arcons on the Bishpool estate in Newport, where many residents have remained in the prefab the occupied when they were first erected.

Uni-Seco

The third most numerous of the THP prefabs was the Uni-Seco or Seco prefab supplied by the Selection Engineering Co. Ltd.[14] With (virtually) flat roofs and corner windows, the Secos were strikingly modern in appearance. What made the Seco system unique was its flexibility: the company designed a 'kit of parts' that could be assembled in various combinations to suit the location and to avoid the monotonous appearance of repetitive rows of prefabs. Seco had produced timber-frame prefabricated-panel emergency huts during the war, and the THP Uni-Seco can be considered as an application of their existing panel system to the Portal design. Timber frames were erected on a concrete or brick plinth, and timber-framed panels of asbestos-cement sheets were screwed on. Wood-wool and wet cement were used as the insulation in the panels, which was claimed to add to the strength of the whole. In practice these weren't as effective as the insulation on Arcons. The panels were protected from the weather with a 'Secomastic' compound, and thin covering strips of asbestos cement were applied over the joints, which added to the temporary feel of the Secos. Even today the surviving examples feel less solid than other prefabs.

The layout of the Uni-Seco Mk III was similar to the universal revised Portal plan that was seen in all of the prefabs, only the hallway was slightly larger. The Seco was unique in that it could be constructed in one of two different forms, giving either a narrow or wide frontage according to how the windows were fitted. Considering that commentators during the development of the prefab prototypes warned against monotonous rows of 'cookie-cutter' housing, it is interesting that only one of the manufacturers explored the benefits of modular prefabrication in this manner. The metal-framed windows were available in

Front Elevation

Side Elevation

45/ The Uni-Seco was a similar size to all the British THP prefabs – 32 feet long by 22 feet wide by 7 feet 6 inches high. 46/ pages 82–83: The corner window of the Uni-Seco was a nod to the non-traditional construction technique. This example in Merlin Close, Bristol, remains a much-loved home.

47/

48/

a variety of glazing-bar configurations (as they were on the Arcons), and other features such as fitted cupboards, ducted hot air from the stove/boiler and kitchen fittings were standard. As with the other prefab types, the internal doors were panelled plywood. The roof was formed, like the frame itself, from timber. Even the cills that sat on the concrete plinths were timber, and it was the decay of these that led to the demise of many of the Secos in the decades after the war. One of the largest estates, at Catford (Lewisham), does remain

47/ Uni-Seco prefabs at Whalebone Lane South in Dagenham. 48/ Uni-Secos at Kings Close, Clapham, in September 1945. Note the original mesh fence, which was used on many prefab estates. 49/ The 100,000th Temporary Housing Programme home, erected in Wandsworth on 29 January 1947. Despite it being one of the coldest weeks of the twentieth century, a crowd turned out to mark the occasion. A sign was erected in front of the prefab to inform passers-by of its significance.

49/

remarkably original, and is a good example of how the two Seco models were combined to prevent monotony. Residents recall how German POWs erected one type, whereas Italians constructed the other.

Tarran
It was obvious to the government from the mid 1940s that they needed Tarran Industries of Hull (and Edinburgh, Leeds and Dundee) in the THP for its experience in prefabrication in the late 1930s and early 1940s, and because the company was already logistically large enough to start production and delivery. It had been Tarran that established Solid Cedar Homes in 1938 and that had erected timber houses in Dundee under the auspices of the 1940 Scottish Special Housing Association.[15] Robert Tarran also regularly invited the press to attend his demonstrations of prefabricated construction, where he would erect single- and two-storey homes in a matter of hours. A series of photographs

showing the building in progress (and time of day written on cards in front of the house, '8 am', '12 noon', '5 pm', etc.) would then appear in the papers for all to marvel at.

Tarran's experience of the (French) Mopin system of concrete prefab panels fixed to a steel frame that was utilised in the construction of the celebrated Quarry Hill flats in 1935 may have given Robert Tarran the confidence he needed to develop his own concrete and steel prefab homes. Nine thousand of Tarran's prefab concrete huts were supplied to the War Department in the first years of the war.[16] A revised version of these huts, the Mk III had a timber roof and 'Lignocrete' panel walls, and this would appear to have been the inspiration for the first of the three Tarran prefab types (all very similar) which were constructed under the Temporary Housing Programme. The 'Lignocrete' trade name referred to the panels which were a mixture of Portland cement concrete, and chemically treated sawdust.

By the summer of 1943 a prototype 'Lignocrete' Tarran bungalow was being exhibited at the Conway Hall in London, and then in Hull. Robert Tarran announced to the press that he could produce some 100,000 such dwellings per annum,[17] though the total figure for Tarrans actually erected under the THP was just over 19,000.

It is interesting to note the interest and enthusiasm that companies like Arcon, Uni-Seco and Tarran invested in the development of their prefabricated temporary homes before they had any official connection with the THP. Such was the energy devoted to the popularisation of prefabs by people like Robert Tarran that one could speculate that even without the THP we would have seen a good number of prefabs erected in Britain (perhaps purchased directly by local authorities). There were so many wartime prefabrication

50/ Tarran prefab at 7 Hopewell Road, Hull, erected in September 1945. This version has a cut-away corner that formed a porch.

51/ Imported American prefab as exhibited at the Tate Gallery on 14 July 1946. Smaller and cheaper to rent than the British prefabs, few seem to have lasted beyond the intended 15-year lifespan.

experiments that the THP can be considered as an agent for making them conform to a uniform pattern.

Such was the public interest in the idea of prefabrication that when Tarran announced a competition to design a 2/3 bedroom house or bungalow using the Tarran system, 131 people made the effort to investigate and submit their ideas.[18] Tarran's own campaigning and publicity stunts to demonstrate the speed with which prefabs could be erected must have gone some way in doing the government's job for them in bringing public attention to the issue. In March 1944 *Picture Post*[19] ran a timely article on Tarran's amazing bungalows that could be 'constructed in six hours', feeding public desire for information and illustration of what was by then a subject of national interest.

Tarran prefab bungalows are almost identical in plan to Uni-Secos, which also meant that they shared some external characteristics. The main differences were that the Tarran had a traditional pitched roof in asbestos concrete panels, and was clad in concrete panels. These gave the Tarran a much more pleasant and solid appearance than the Uni-Seco. On the other hand these concrete panels made the Tarran the heaviest of the prefabs, at 14 tons (most other types were just 8 tons). It may have been this that explained why the majority of Tarrans were constructed in the north of England and in Scotland, close to the centres of production.

USA (imported)

Considering the US inspiration for much of the Portal design (inside and out), and the attention that all the books on prefabrication as a technique had given to the American examples,[20] it isn't surprising that the government decided to import some US prefabs for construction in Britain. Plans were made to import

30,000 under Lend Lease, though when Lend Lease arrangements were cut short this figure was reduced to 8000. The US prefabs were timber-frame units and arrived as seven flat-packed panels faced in either fibreboard or asbestos cement sheets. The roof was also formed from prefab sections, and had a shallow pitch. Reflecting the US origins of the panels, each one was certified guaranteed against termite attack,[21] but the bungalows still had to be painted to prevent them rotting.

The US prefabs were slightly smaller than the average UK prefab (24 feet 2 inches – 7.4 metres – square) and generally had a shorter life because their construction was unsuitable for the UK climate. Their size meant that councils offered them at slightly lower rates than the other prefab types. The floor plan

52/ Alan Crowe was given a photo-tinting set for his eleventh birthday, and set about hand-colouring photos that he had taken of his imported US prefab.

differed from the typical Portal-inspired layout of the UK prefabs, having the hall (for a pram) at one side of the building, rather than centrally. The toilet was located in the bathroom, and the kitchen had a gas cooker (which came as part of the US-imported package). In common with the majority of prefab types (apart from Aluminium Bungalows), the US bungalows were given unused Anderson shelters as garden sheds. The UK government added a wash boiler with an immersion heater for hot water in the summer. Later models appear to have been given all-UK fittings in an attempt to reduce transport costs from the USA.

The media liked the idea that we were importing whole houses from America, and soon some people thought that the whole THP was a US import. The fact that all the prefabs looked so different to traditional housing may be the reason that this rumour spread so effectively. Even today, people living in British-made prefabs claim that they are living in 'Americans', and the prestige accruing from the perception that their homes were something extra special has remained. Certainly, things like fully fitted kitchens were popular earlier in America than they were in Britain (and would have been seen in Hollywood films) and so it was natural for many to assume that they were indeed living in an imported home.

In contrast to many of the UK prefabs – actually semi-permanent or permanent/demountable homes that were only 'Temporary' by virtue of their construction under the THP – the US-imported prefabs were genuinely temporary as their construction was limited to a decade or so of life. None appears to have survived into the twenty-first century, and it is likely that all were demolished by the mid 1960s.

53/

Spooner

Hull produced not only the three Tarran variants, but also the less common Spooner prefab.[23] J L Spooner's 'Dri-Built' system of plywood panels between timber frames was employed in the construction of temporary and permanent homes. Despite the national timber shortage, the windows were also timber, and the roof was felt-covered plywood. Even the inside had a plywood finish. Internally the Spooners followed the Portal plan with a Ministry of Works 'heart' unit. Only 2000 of these plywood 'boxes' were constructed under the THP, and they do not appear to have been particularly long-lived. Being built of ply, the original intention was for the exterior to have been painted in the first instance, and for a brick skin to be added to the bungalows when labour was available. Other Spooner THP bungalows that were constructed during periods of particular timber shortage appear to have been clad in aluminium alloy sheet (such as a group in Sheffield), or 20g steel sheets with asbestos-cement sheet

54/ 55/

roofs. These tended to use standard steel casement windows. Permanent Spooners were also built, of semi-detached and detached construction.

Universal

With experience in constructing more than a thousand non-traditional partially prefabricated homes between 1925 and 1928, the Universal Housing Co. Ltd of Rickmansworth was a natural choice to construct temporary homes under the THP. Steel frames and roof trusses were clad with asbestos-cement

53/ Spooner prefab at Colchester in November 1946. Because the later Spooners (such as this one) were constructed around metal tube frames, they had rounded corners. 54/ Universal prefab at Buckleigh Road, Streatham, London in April 1946. Universal Engineering Ltd of Rickmansworth produced these asbestos-clad homes. 55/ Ms Munday in the garden of her Universal prefab in 1960.

sheets which were attached to timber-framed panels. The roof was given asbestos-cement corrugated sheeting. Two thousand Universals were erected under the THP, but it appears that only one survives today and this has been reconstructed at the Chiltern Museum.

Phoenix

The Phoenix bungalow rivals the Mk V Arcon for its cottagey looks; Olde England rising from the ashes of war. With a traditional panelled timber front door identical to those used on Tudorbethan homes of the 1930s, and a recognisable chimney raised above the pitched roofline, the Phoenix was one of the more homely looking prefab types.

The architects of contractors John Laing, McAlpine and Henry Boot Ltd appear to have been behind the design of this timber-framed, asbestos-clad prefab home.[22] In common with the majority of prefab types, floors were of timber joist and floorboard over a concrete slab, and the roof was supported by steel portal frames. Internally the layout is similar to Tarrans and later Uni-Secos, with the minor difference that the door from the hall to the living room was central on the wall (potentially wasting space). Like the Orlit and Miller prefabs, the Phoenixes were not as prefabricated as their more numerous Aluminium, Arcon, Tarran and Seco counterparts. Of the 2500 that were built, the Phoenixes generally fared well, with one group in Moseley surviving in good enough condition to become, in July 1998, the first listed THP prefabs.

56/ Residents at 423 Wake Green Road, Birmingham in 1999. The Phoenix prefabs were all fitted with traditional 'cottage' panelled wooden front doors.

Orlit

Little is known of the 255 THP Orlit bungalows as they do not appear to have been recorded in the contemporary press. What we do know is that the firm was founded in 1940 and is known for its wartime concrete hutments as well as permanent prefabricated two-storey houses after the THP. It is unclear if the THP Orlit bungalows resembled their wartime huts or not, but we can be sure that the system was based on a prefabricated concrete frame, and it is likely that they had precast concrete roof and floor members and were also clad with concrete slabs. The author has been unable to trace any photographs of this prefab type.

Miller

Like the Orlit prefabs, there do not appear to be surviving photographs of original-condition Miller bungalows, of which just 100 were erected (in Scotland) under the THP in 1946. All of the Millers were of concrete construction, which was formed *in-situ* using reusable shuttering, so were not particularly prefabricated. The outside of these concrete panels was rendered, and hardboard was added to the interior. Internal walls were one of the few prefab elements, and were of hardboard attached to a timber frame. Timber was also used for the roof which was clad with asbestos cement sheets.

Isle of Lewis

The most expensive of the THP prefabs was the Isle of Lewis model, and only 50 were constructed. The increased costs came from the need to redesign the prefab to make it withstand the extreme weather conditions on the Hebrides, and also to ship in the prefabricated concrete blocks and the labour force.

Apart from the heavyweight construction, the Isle of Lewis bungalows apparently followed the typical Portal two-bedroomed bungalow design. Enquiries have not brought any photos to light.

An early end ...

The Temporary Housing Programme did not provide the instant homes at low prices that it had originally promised. Costs spiralled as the programme progressed; with the whole project costing over £200 million, and providing 100,000 fewer homes than had been projected for the original estimated cost of £150 million.[24] Under the project a total of 156,623 prefabricated homes were erected between 1945 and 1949.[25] Other permanent prefab types were being constructed and imported at the same time, and continued to be produced into the decades that followed. Table 1 on page 100 lists the various types and their costs.

It was primarily spiralling costs that led to the early demise of the programme, but other factors were Lend Lease changes that led to the end of US prefab imports (the cheapest bungalow type), and the return of the prisoners of war who had provided labour to their own countries in 1947. The people who moved into prefab homes in the late 1940s would not have cared about the costs of programme or the fact that the THP had failed in what it had set out to achieve. What mattered to these people was the fact that they had comfortable spacious new homes with all mod cons.

58/

57/ 425 Wake Green Road in Birmingham, one of a row of Grade II-listed Phoenix prefabs. 58/ The only other Phoenix prefabs to have survived are in Bristol, including this example at Blackswarth Road in Brislington.

Prefab Types and Costs in 1948[26]

Prefab type	Number constructed	Cost per unit (December 1947)	Total cost (nearest thousand)
Aluminium Bungalow (B2)	54,500	£1610	£87,745,000
Arcon Mk V	38,859	£1209	£46,981,000
Uni-Seco	28,999	£1131	£32,798,000
Tarran*	1015	£1022	£1,037,000
Tarran*	11,000	£1147	£12,617,000
Tarran*	6999	£1126	£7,881,000
USA (imported)	8462	£663	£5,610,000
Phoenix	2428	£1200	£2,914,000
Spooner	2000	£1079	£2,158,000
Universal	2000	£1218	£2,436,000
Orlit	255	£1202	£307,000
Miller	100	£1139	£114,000
Isle of Lewis	50	£2000	£100,000
Total	156,667		£202,698,000

* Three different types of Tarran were constructed under the THP. The original source does not identify the types.

[1] Joad 1943; page 94, requoted in Vale 1995.
[2] See Field 1991.
[3] See Robins 2001.
[4] Burnett 1978, page 258.
[5] See Jackson 1973, Stevenson 2002.
[6] See Finnemore 1985 for a detailed study of the Aluminium Bungalow.
[7] Madge 1946, page 215.
[8] Finnemore 1982, page 15, and supported by Vale 1990.
[9] 'Production of prefabricated aluminium houses', in the *Journal of the RIBA*, July 1946.
[10] Squire 1984, page 96, cited in Vale 1990; page 243.
[11] Arcon 1948, page 78.
[12] Arcon 1948, page 80.
[13] But all are planned for demolition by 2005, including those currently in private ownership.
[14] Uni-Secos are known as Secos in Scotland.
[15] Bowley 1966, page 212; cited in Vale 1995, page 11.
[16] Rankine 1942, page 218.
[17] Neel 1943, page 212.
[18] 'The Tarran House' page 110 in *The Builder*, 11 August 1944.
[19] 4 March 1944, pages 18–19.
[20] For further reading on US wartime and post-war prefabs see Burkhart B, A Arieff 2002, Columbia River Exhibition undated, Fetters 2002, Harrison *et al* 1945.
[21] 'Temporary Houses from the USA', pages 143–4 in *Architectural Design and Construction*, June 1945.
[22] *The Builder*, 9 March 1945, page 201.
[23] Information on the Spooner, Orlit, Miller and Isle of Lewis prefab types is from Vale 1990.
[24] *Parliamentary Papers 1956–57*, Vol. 20, page 441.
[25] *Parliamentary Papers 1948–49*, Vol. 22, page 420.
[26] Statistics from Works, 1948, page 2. Note that the total number of prefabs listed is slightly greater than the 156,623 which were actually constructed, at a slightly higher cost of £207,309,000. These final figures can be found in *Parliamentary Papers 1948–49*, Vol. 22, page 420.

59/ The early 1950s-style lounge of an Aluminium Bungalow reconstructed at the Museum of Welsh Life.

prefab interiors/

Homes are built to live in, and not to look on …
Francis Bacon

Moving into a home with electric lighting and sockets, a plumbed-in internal bathroom and toilet, hot water on tap, a wash boiler, cooker and refrigerator was an exciting event for the original occupants of Britain's post-war prefabs. To have moved from rented 'rooms' where people often had to share a toilet, bathing and cooking facilities with other families, to having all the latest mod cons for oneself was a memorable occasion.

> I will never forget my joy at first seeing our lovely house – the built-in cupboards, wardrobes etc, were unbelievable. After living with my parents and two daughters, plus my husband and brother (after their demob), it was heaven! /Ruth Haynes, who moved into her Aluminium Bungalow in 1947

Even today one of the first things that residents recall of their first days in their prefab was their wonder at new home technologies. Friends and family would visit to survey the interior fittings or take advantage of the bathroom facilities (as late as 1951 a third of British households was still without a plumbed-in bath). Many were envious of the fact that prefabs had fridges, as few could afford such luxuries.

> It had a fitted fridge, a kitchen table that folded into the wall, and a bathroom. Friends and family came visiting to view the wonders. It seemed like living in a spaceship. /Neil Kinnock, the former Labour Party leader, who lived in an Arcon Mk V from 1947 to 1961[1]

> My mother was very proud of the prefab with its fitted kitchen that included a refrigerator. She was keen to replace any old-fashioned furniture with what she called 'contemporary' pieces in keeping with her modern home. /Margaret Sinnott

So great was curiosity in the contents of these futuristic homes that a Pontypool man was arrested for peering into a bungalow. 'I have never seen inside a prefab and I just wanted to take a look' was his defence.[2]

The compulsion to 'keep up with the times' had been the driving force behind the consumption of a whole host of new domestic appliances in the interwar years, but in the prefab these goods were supplied for the first time by the government. Prefab homes had so many fitted cupboards that residents didn't have to buy storage furniture, and kitchen shelves came equipped with pots and pans.

> So many cupboards. Including the airing cupboard where we used to hide when there was a thunder storm – after turning the mirrors to the wall, of course. /Edna Pound recalling her 1950s Uni-Seco childhood at Pound Hill in Guildford

It isn't surprising that some felt that the prefab represented the new Britain that they had been fighting for in World War 2.

60/ The lounge of a Tarran prefab photographed in September 1945. Virtually all the furnishings date from the 1930s. 61/ page 106: The kitchen of the Aluminium Bungalow reconstructed at the Museum of Welsh Life. Note the shelf inset into the wall that contains the plumbing 'heart' unit. 62/ page 107: The cupboard under the sink in the kitchen would have been used to store cleaning products.

61/

/palaces for the people/

> The bath was a luxury early in 1947, also having a flush toilet in those days was
> really great, and inside the bathroom! With an electric cooker, electric washing
> facilities and a fridge, it was lovely after coming home from the War.
> /Mr R H Clements

Not everyone would have been familiar with the new technologies offered by the prefab – after all, a quarter of British homes were still without a mains electricity supply.[3] To enable them to take advantage of the 'efficiency' and 'freedom' that electricity could bring to their lives a booklet was provided for all new residents, *Electric Service in Temporary Houses*. This explained how the Ministry of Works had designed the control panels especially so that in the kitchen a single panel controlled the main electricity supply, the cooker, immersion heater, kettle, fuses and light switch.[4] Photographs showed how the drop-down table made an ideal ironing board.

> The internal wiring had arrived pre-cut and had been installed by unskilled
> technicians. They must have done something wrong because at first everything
> worked fine, but only if you left the hall light on. /Mrs Peggy Dobbs, who remains
> in her Newport Arcon after 56 years

Each prefab was provided with six electric-power points – two in the kitchen, two in the living room, and one in each bedroom. This was considered a generous allocation. It was anticipated that they would be used for electric

63/ The kitchen in Mrs Tinsley's Uni-Seco, Clapham, in September 1945. The rack above the stove is in use for drying crockery.

65/

66/

64/ Detail of the folding kitchen rack fitted in Aluminium Bungalows and Uni-Secos. Plates would be placed here to dry with the heat from the cooker. 65/ The original electric cooker at 57 The Crapen, Cam, Gloucestershire, still working well in 1996, after half a century of service. 66/ The kitchen of 57 The Crapen in 1996. It is remarkable how many of the prefabs that survived into the 1990s retained complete and original 1940s interiors. Mrs Elsie Fowler lived at 57 The Crapen in Cam from the time of its erection in 1948 until 1996. She kept the kitchen immaculate and original in the hope that it might one day be moved to a museum. Sadly, it was demolished with the rest of the estate.

68/

heaters, kettle, iron, vacuum cleaner, toaster, table and floor standard lamps, electric clocks and a wireless. In practice only about a third of households would have had appliances such as vacuum cleaners, but irons and toasters were already common.

The cooker would have been much more advanced than those that most people had been used to, with an oven, separate grill, two hotplates, and a 'SIM' control for simmering. A multi-fuel stove – the only source of heat in the house – was fitted in the living room.

67/ Mrs Rhys John and her kitten keeping cool by sitting on the air conditioner in her Kuwait Arcon. 68/ The kitchen of an Arcon erected at Ahmadi in Kuwait, photographed in 1953. Note the water filter above the sink, and a coal bin where most had a wash-boiler.

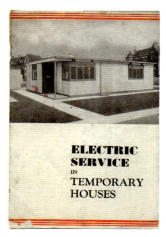

69/

> The best memory I have is the metal stove in the living room...we could burn anything in it, and therefore had very little rubbish for the bin man. /June Sowerby

A back boiler was fitted to the fire to heat water, with an immersion heater for use in the summer. Many Arcons were initially fitted with 'Siesta' fires, but these proved inadequate and were replaced with a red-enamelled model.

> The chimney had to be swept every six weeks, and my father had to don a boiler suit and go up on the roof. All furniture near the fireplace had to be covered. /Jean Connell

69/ *Electric Service in Temporary Houses*, a booklet given to all prefab residents, featuring the Uni-Seco prototype that had been exhibited at the Tate Gallery. 70/ The electric cooker and wash-boiler as fitted in Aluminium Bungalows and Uni-Secos.

The Electric Cooker with the Wash Boiler beside it, beneath the draining-board, as fitted in earlier types of house.

The Electric Cooker.

The electric cooker has been designed for the temporary house and is capable of cooking all meals for an average family.

The quick heating oven has thermostatic control with the heat indication marked in degrees Fahrenheit. It is only necessary to turn the control knob to the desired temperature to bring the oven up to the required heat. A red light shows behind the control knob when the current is on. As soon as the oven is hot the light goes out but comes on again intermittently while the oven is in use. The cooker instruction card gives the correct settings for roasting and baking as well as other useful hints.

The Circular Boiling Plate on top of the cooker can be used for all ordinary purposes, but for boiling water an electric kettle is usually more economical. The boiling plate switch gives four heat positions: the lowest, marked "SIM", keeps a large pan simmering. Never leave the boiling plate switched on without a pan covering it.

Under the draining board stood an electric or gas wash boiler that held 10 gallons of hot water and clothes.

> I can remember fixing my small rubber wringer on the top of the copper and wringing my washing straight into the sink, filled with 'Blue' rinsing water – Bliss! At the end of the sink was the refrigerator – my first ever! /Ruth Haynes

The refrigerator had a capacity of 3 cubic feet, which was considered 'ample for the storage of all the perishable food needed by an average household'. Residents were reminded that refrigerators were best used all year round, and not just in hot weather. Those prefabs that had gas connected had mains gas cookers, wash boilers and fridges, and if the pilot lights went out residents had to relight them with a match. People were encouraged to use electric kettles rather than the cooker for boiling water (many would previously have cooked on coal-fired ranges), and to conserve electricity whenever possible.

The prefab interior was simple and utilitarian. Everything was well designed, well proportioned and well thought-out. No space went to waste, and cupboards were fitted in every available place with the kind of ingenuity that one would expect to find in caravan design. Several prefab types enjoyed large picture windows or novel corner windows and doors that led directly into gardens. Where possible, prefabs were erected with the main façade facing south, so the bungalows enjoyed sun throughout the day.

Kitchens and bathrooms were designed with contemporary concerns about hygiene and efficiency in mind, and had fitted work surfaces in the kitchen and fitted boards around the bath. In line with then-current thinking about kitchen design, there was minimal distance between the preparation, cooking and washing areas. The prefab really did enable a new way of living, breaking down old assumptions about home design, providing single-storey living with all mod cons and no wasted space such as parlours or grandiose hallways.

> We were delighted when we were allocated No. 2 Park Place. No more standing over the old coal range and having the job of black-leading it for my mother. No more having to keep the milk in a bucket of cold water in the summer. No more trips outside to the toilet in the cold and dark. Never again would we have to use the tin bath in front of the fire, and there was no need to heat the water in a bucket on the range. /Mrs A V Ellis recalling the new way of living in her Treherbert prefab in the Rhondda Valley

Prefab interiors reflected growing public consciousness about design and the importance of 'good' design in the home. The innovative use of limited space with minimal decorative detailing and the functional design of fittings appealed to contemporary design critics.[5] Gone were the fussy pastiche historical interiors of the 1930s that so irritated people like Nikolaus Pevsner and Anthony Bertram, to be replaced by utilitarian design that had more than a hint of interwar modernism about it. In fact the immediate post-war books pro-

71/ page 118: An Aluminium Bungalow bathroom in original condition. 'The bath was a luxury in 1947, also having a flush toilet in those days was really great, and inside the bathroom! ... it was lovely after coming home from the war.' Mr R H Clements. 72/ page 119: The fitted mirror and hand basin in a Gloucestershire Aluminium Bungalow, photographed in 1996.

moting prefabrication featured photographs of the living room of Ernö Goldfinger's modernist house in Willow Road, Hampstead, alongside images of prefab interiors.[6]

Decorating
When people learned that they had been successful in their application for a prefab, they were instructed to go to it straight away and put curtains up at the windows as any apparently empty property meant that the housing office would be inundated with enquiries.

> Imagine our pleasure when we heard we would be allocated a prefab. He said, 'Move in as quickly as possible, before the squatters do.' We did just that, ordering furniture, bedding and lino squares from Mr Small's Outfitters on Stratford Road. /Henry Dodwell, who moved into his Edgbaston prefab a week before the heavy snows of January 1947

External doors and windows were painted according to a limited palette supplied by the Ministry of Works. Inside, residents had more freedom to decorate, although few would have had the surplus money for such a luxury until the 1950s. Prefabs were ready-decorated in magnolia when residents moved in. The rooms often had their pine floorboards finished with a dark 'Jacobean' varnish around the edges and residents added linoleum sporting either traditional floral or modern geometric motifs. The 'linos' had to be polished regularly to keep them in good condition.

> We couldn't afford carpet so I cut up an imitation fur coat and made it into a rug for

> in front of the fire. /Emily Stephens, who moved into her prefab in Hall Green, Birmingham, in April 1946

Rugs would have been either traditional hand-made rag-rugs, coconut matting, or, if recently purchased, may have used cubist-inspired geometric patterning.

> We enjoyed decorating the prefab, and I wallpapered our bedrooms and panelled the living room with the help of my next door neighbour. It felt quite posh.
> /Ruth Haynes

Residents were supposed to ask permission before decorating, but very few did. It was understood that anything which the council deemed unsightly when the occupier moved out would be reversed – either by the occupier or by the council. If the council did any work the old tenant would be billed.

By the mid 1950s tenants were replacing internal panelled doors with the fashionable flush variety, sometimes with glamorous handles moulded from resin and incorporating glitter.

> I remember my dad with a paint brush and two pots of paint, dabbing it on the living-room wall, making a pattern because they couldn't afford wallpaper in 1945. Later on they came up in the world, and papered every room. /Margaret Sprakes

73/ page 122: Detail of the hand basin in an Aluminium Bungalow. 76/ page 123: Detail of the kitchen sink of an Aluminium Bungalow. Having hot water on tap was a luxury that few residents would have enjoyed before they moved into their prefab.

74/

75/

76/

75/ The second bedroom as furnished in the Aluminium Bungalow reconstructed at the Museum of Welsh Life. Typically, two children would have shared this room. 76/ The lounge of an Arcon exported for British oil workers in Kuwait, photographed in 1953. The oil company provided the luxury furnishings, purchased from Waring & Gillow. Most prefab residents in Britain would not have had such fine quality furniture. 77/ The multi-fuel stove as fitted in US-imported prefabs in Southampton. 78/ The original fire in an Aluminium Bungalow, still in good working order when photographed in 1996.

77/ 78/

Paint would have been the most common wall treatment, but by the mid 1950s many residents were wallpapering at least some of the rooms.

> The vertical metal laths between wall sections made decorating a nightmare. Mum and dad tried painting the laths and papering in-between, but in the end concluded that the laths looked better papered. They used to paste on a board balanced on two Utility chairs in the kitchen, and I played houses underneath. /Mary Sprakes

Wallpapers came in a tremendous range of patterns, from the traditional floral to the garishly modern, but as with carpets and soft furnishings, the most popular colours for wallpapers were brown and cream 'autumn tints'. Plain papers, washable papers, flock, textured and embossed were available.

> Before the prefab living room was wallpapered every three or four years it would

79/   80/

be my bit of fun to put a sharp pencil down both sides of the 'alu band' which joined the sections. This was great fun for a kid who waited patiently for the last few years to do it. In 1963 we redecorated my bedroom, and being Beatles mad I wanted Beatles wallpaper. Mum could not afford it so I settled for smaller bits of wallpaper. They were sold separately and were about 18 x 24 inches. They were in fact bits of Beatles wallpaper cut off a roll. /Ken Wakefield, recalling his childhood in a Southampton aluminium bungalow

79/ Pauline and Christine Valente in the lounge of their Arcon, 1959. By this time the family had wallpapered the painted walls, and had acquired a carpet square for the floor. 80/ A 1953 party in an Arcon in Kuwait. Note the luxury furnishings and modern wireless. 81/ Christine and Sharon Page in the lounge of their Newport Arcon, 1960. Sharon's school uniform hangs on the fitted cupboards, as the children listen to their favourite programme on the wireless.

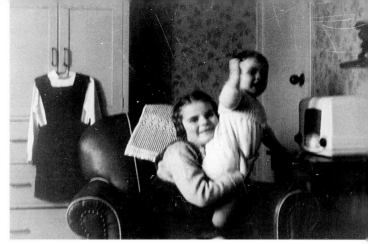

81/

Furnishings

Many prefab residents had to find new furniture as they were moving out of accommodation that was either shared with their family or furnished tenements. However, most people found new furnishings prohibitively expensive. The fitted cupboards, larder, airing cupboard and drop-down table provided in Arcons and Uni-Secos would have saved some purchases (and few had to buy wardrobes), but chairs, a dining table and beds were required. Many spent weeks with almost no furniture as they waited for the essential coupon or 'docket' for Utility-brand purchases.

Utility furniture

When customers visited department stores to purchase new furnishings they were not met with the vast array of interior styles that they would have had before 1939. In fact they may have seen very little furniture at all, as even the

82/ George Page in an Arcon at Treberth in Newport, 1960. Note the fitted cupboards, and the mix of furnishings dating from the 1930s to the 1950s. George's family remained in this prefab until it was demolished in 2002.

government-organised Utility-brand furniture was in short supply, and shops were not given samples to display. Utility furniture was originally supplied exclusively to those who had been bombed out and those who were setting up new homes, although the nursery range was available to anyone. Customers were allocated 60 coupons, and could decide how they spent them: a chair was one docket, a wardrobe was eight. Orders came directly from one of hundreds of local factories once a coupon had been received; thus shops attempted to persuade their customers to leave their purchases with them for a few days or even weeks so that others could see the goods.

This experiment in standardisation and mass production makes an interesting parallel with the THP. The 22 standardised designs in the wartime range made careful use of limited timber; only one item (introduced in 1945) was produced in metal. There had been several popular brands of tubular steel and other metal furniture in the 1930s, and this could have been another opportunity for the government to engage the enlarged steel and aluminium industries. But Utility-brand furniture was made of oak or mahogany.

The Utility scheme had been introduced in August 1942 for a variety of textiles and clothes. In October 1942 the Utility Furniture Exhibition opened in London, and was visited by 30,000 people in the three weeks that it was open. The Utility Furniture Advisory Committee used Gordon Russell to oversee the furniture designs 'to ensure a supply of furniture of the best quality available at controlled prices to meet a real need'.[7] Having a recognised designer was useful for associating the Utility brand with good-quality workmanship. Two consumer representatives joined the panel, the Reverend Charles Jenkinson and Mrs E Winborn who represented 'the ordinary housewife'. Edwin Clinch, H T Cutler and L J Barnes were the designers.

UTILITY FURNITURE

LIVING ROOM

SIDEBOARD: Second Section—Model 1a
Price £10.7.0

The living room furniture is in oak. The dining chairs have loose, padded seats covered with leather cloth, in a variety of colours.

SIDEBOARD: Second Section—Model 1b
Price £10.7.0

Sideboard, with doors open, showing inside shelves. The sideboards are 4 ft. wide, 2 ft. 9 ins. high and 1 ft. 6 ins. deep.

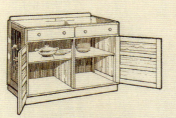

DINING CHAIR:
Second Section—Model 3a
Price £1.9.0

DINING CHAIR:
Second Section—Model 3c
Price £1.9.0

83/ A page from a Utility furniture catalogue issued by the Board of Trade on 1 January 1943. 84/ Utility dining chair in oak. Seat covers came in various colours.

84/

The first Utility furniture catalogue appeared on New Year's Day 1943, and was divided into sections for the various rooms of the house. The furniture was utilitarian in design, solidly constructed, plain, functional and well detailed. Veneered boards were used for all panels, all joints were morticed or pegged, and plastic was banned from the handles and fittings. Because of this adherence to traditional English furniture construction it isn't surprising that the resulting designs bear more than a passing resemblance to late Arts and Crafts designs, or the 1930s Quaker-built furniture from Brynmawr.

For Gordon Russell the scheme represented an opportunity to patronise the furniture buying public, and show them the benefits of 'good' design. The Board of Trade proposed that the scheme should be 'influencing popular taste towards good construction in simple, agreeable designs to the benefit of our after-the-war homes'. Thus Utility furniture contrasts with the reproduction pieces that had been popular before World War 2. Like the prefabs themselves, Utility furniture provided an opportunity for the government to educate the public towards 'better taste', and as such were examples of totalitarian design.

From 1946 Utility furniture became more generally available, and not just to those with permits. The second Utility furniture catalogue was published in 1947, and included the new Cotswold and Chiltern ranges as well as Lloyd Loom-type furniture which was 'off ration'. By this time some Utility furniture was being produced abroad, and there was an increasing use of aluminium.

Although rationing of furniture ended in June 1948, Utility furniture continued in production, with manufacturers now free to add their own designs under the Utility stamp. This meant that they were free of purchase tax and price-control. The Tories eventually forced the end of the successful scheme in January 1953, viewing it as a vestige of wartime socialism to be stamped out.

Britain Can Make It

In September 1946 the *Britain Can Make It* exhibition was organised by the Council of Industrial Design (CoID), and held at the Victoria & Albert Museum.[8] Its aim was to represent the best of British goods that would help with reconstruction. Manufacturers were encouraged to be more adventurous in the design of domestic appliances, furniture, tableware, carpets, wallpaper, clothing, packaging and toys. Wedgwood featured architect Keith Murray's ceramic designs, but few prefab dwellers would have had the funds to afford such luxuries. More than 1.5 million people visited the exhibition in just three months, eager to see the 'look' of the new world they had been fighting for.

As with Utility-brand goods, the exhibition promoted the concept of 'good' design. The CoID appointed itself as arbiter of that which was 'good', and generally looked to the pre-war innovations of modernist designers and the idea that 'form follows function'. Many commercially successful products were rejected by the CoID for inclusion in the exhibition, illustrating the difference between its taste and that of the public. Throughout the late 1940s posters and pamphlets were produced encouraging people to dispose of their fussy, decorated objects from the interwar period and purchase the new Utility-branded goods. This thinly veiled attempt to kick-start post-war industries was not always appreciated by the industries themselves, who felt oppressed by the 'left-wing, centralising ambitions' of a government that enforced sterile Utility design.[9] In the event many of the designs exhibited in the exhibition proved to be for export only, giving rise to the alternative title, *Britain Can't Have It*.

Austerity style

Despite the noble intentions of the Utility scheme and the advice of the CoID, the majority of prefabs would not have been filled with well-designed modern furniture. People made do with whatever they could get, and even those with money to buy new furniture would have brought some older pieces with them.

> Our living room furniture was what my parents bought at the time of their marriage in the 1930s. There was a dining table with flaps that pulled out; it was solid oak and quite classy looking. We also had a small three-piece suite that looked like leather, but it was something called 'Rexene'. Some things were given to them as they lost furniture in the bombing. Oh yes, and the sideboard, that was a must. /Patricia Skeels

Magazines gave tips on how to renovate furniture in the modern style, and many would have had the skills to repair or make their own pieces. If second-hand furniture was used it was most likely to have been made in the prolific 1930s, and on a smaller scale to the Victorian and Edwardian designs that preceded it. This interwar furniture was often constructed out of cheap softwoods (and much plywood) and veneered in oak or jazz-modern patterns in exotic fruitwoods.

> We came from a couple of rented rooms which were furnished so we had no furniture. I think my two grans and other family members gave most of it. We kept that furniture until quite late, perhaps around 1960 or so. The furniture was almost all 1930s. The sofa and chairs were big boxy things with big curved arms, [they were] dark green. The only other furniture I can remember was the bedroom furniture. The wardrobes, for instance, were dark stained with three arched doors, typical thirties stuff. In the early sixties there was more money around so the furniture was replaced.
> /Ken Wakefield

When money was short people didn't worry about holistic interior design, and modern prefab interiors would often have been home to interwar historical pastiche styles, as well as the more suitable 'Streamline Moderne' or 'Jazz-Modern' pieces. Very often the home would happily combine incongruous styles, and dining tables that harked back to a romantic vision of the past would stand next to a functionalist Utility sideboard. The recycled interwar furniture was often a confusion of styles itself, the very stuff that appalled designers like Gordon Russell. Oak-veneer furniture often blended modernistic outlines with cabriole or barley-twist legs. Even those who had the 'Odeon'-styled boxy three-piece suites often covered them with lace antimacassars!

The essential wireless cabinets and speaker boxes more often than not adopted the modern style, and were commonly 1930s examples decorated with fretwork panels depicting stylised images of the sun rising.[10] Some even found space for a piano. Poorly proportioned oak cabinets, tables and sideboards haphazardly blended impersonations of decorative styles from the fifteenth to the seventeenth centuries. Particularly common were bulbous Jacobean-styled legs on sideboards and dining suites. These suited well the half-timbered mock-historical boarding on the exterior and interiors of many interwar suburban homes, but were incongruous in the functional prefab interior.

[1] 'When I was a child', *Daily Mail*, 26 September 1986.
[2] Recounted in Robins 2001, page 8.
[3] Barrett and Phillips 1987, page 156.
[4] On all THP prefabs apart from the imported American model.
[5] See Robertson 1947.
[6] Association of Building Technicians 1946, photo 4.
[7] Further reading on Utility furniture in Dover 1991 and Hillier 1975.
[8] Further reading in Sparke 1986 and the Council of Industrial Design 1946.
[9] McLaren 1997, page 6.
[10] See Forty 1972.

> The art of architecture studies not structure itself, but the effect of structure on the human spirit.
> *Geoffrey Scott*

'We are all middle class now'

The prefabs estates became lands of opportunity for those moving from rooms in rented Victorian terraces to houses on large detached plots on the outskirts of towns.

> The space is what I remember most. We were moving from an area of mostly terraced houses with backyards and little space for a kid to run around, and going to this sea of white prefabs with gardens and trees on large greens. As far as I was concerned I was moving to the countryside. /Ken Wakefield, who grew up in an Aluminium Bungalow on the outskirts of Southampton

For many of the young couples moving into a prefab, their new home represented the 'bright, new' future that they had imagined the post-war world would be. The building itself, with fitted cupboards and novel design had personality.

> Some of my happiest memories are of living in my 'beautiful prefab', especially after living through the Second World War, and all of us surviving. /Ruth Haynes, recalling life in a Plymouth Aluminium Bungalow 1947–57

85/ Muriel Adder and baby Mary photographed in 1951 in front of their prefab shed, a wartime Anderson shelter.

86/

138/

87/ 88/

It was a new way of living, with space for separate bedrooms, indoor conveniences and adequate modern appliances to make life easier. Like the buildings themselves, the generation of '20-somethings' and their children were remarkably uniform.

> We felt that we were part of something new and exciting. The estate absolutely

86/ Alan Page, aged 19, photographed in the garden of his Arcon on the Treberth estate, Newport, in 1953. Although the prefab was demolished in 2002 Alan still lives in one of the modern bungalows built to replace his former home. 87/ Mr and Mrs Wakefield under the canopy at the side entrance to their Southampton Aluminium Bungalow in 1958. They lived at 84 Orpen Road, and Mrs Wakefield's mother and father lived in another prefab at No. 94. 88/ Dennis Valente and daughter Pauline outside their Birmingham Arcon in 1957, a decade after they moved in.

swarmed with young kids, and the joy that we got from all those open fields, streams and 'real' adventure playgrounds is something I will never forget.
/Jill Shilvock

Despite the restrictions on post-war life, the prefab represented almost 'utopian' living. Everyone was experiencing new technologies together, people had more space than ever before, and austerity measures such as rationing were a shared experience. The country had been drawn together in the war, and for many the prefab estates were a continuation of that communal experience. For some it felt like they were permanently living in a holiday camp. Few would say that their prefab days were anything but the best days of their lives.

I had no idea that I lived in a glorified shack when I was little, because lots of us did. I thought we were quite rich compared to some kids at school, which we were in our way. I was always clean and wore good shoes. /Mary Sprakes

For the first time in British history there was real uniformity and standardisation, not only in the homes that people lived in and the furnishings in their home, but also in the clothes that they wore, and the food that they ate. 'We are all middle class now' proclaimed politicians, and the war had certainly blurred divisions between the classes. Council-provided prefab homes were furnished with luxury goods such as refrigerators that had been the exclusive preserve of the middle classes before 1939.

When asked about what made prefab life so special, most residents refer to the sense of community that they experienced on their estate. The unique circumstances that brought together hundreds of people who had much in

89/ A Cardiff family standing proudly in front of their Mk V Arcon.

EXTRACTS from TENANCY AGREEMENT.

1. **THE TENANT SHALL NOT:—**
   (a) Use the premises as a shop, workshop, or business premises, or advertise thereon;
   (b) Sublet or take in lodgers;
   (c) Erect any shed or other building on the premises or
   (d) Keep any animals or birds on the premises, except with the written consent of the Corporation.

2. **In no case is linoleum or similar material to be used on any wooden floors on the ground floor.**

3. The tenant is to cultivate and manage the garden in a proper manner and is to make good any damage to the premises (including windows and sanitary fittings) caused otherwise than by ordinary wear and tear.

4. **The tenancy may be terminated by either party giving one week's previous notice in writing, expiring on a Monday—(The Keys should be delivered at the HOUSING BUREAU, 17 CORN STREET, NEWPORT, or to the Collector, before 12 noon on the day the notice expires).**

Summary of Sec. 58, 59 and 61 of the Housing Act, 1936.

1. After the First day of July, 1937, an occupier who causes or permits his dwelling to be overcrowded is liable to prosecution for an offence under the Housing Act, 1936, and if convicted, to a fine not exceeding five pounds. Any part of a house which is occupied by a separate family is a "dwelling."

2. A dwelling is overcrowded if the number of persons sleeping in it is more than the "permitted number," or is such that two or more of those persons, being ten years old or over, of opposite sexes (not being persons living together as husband and wife), must sleep in the same room.

3. The "permitted number" for the dwelling to which this Rent Card relates is ...... 6 ...... persons.

In counting the number of persons each child under ten years of age counts as half a person, and a child of less than one year is not counted at all.

4. The Act contains special provisions relating to overcrowding already existing on the above-mentioned date or which is due to a child attaining the age of either one or ten years after that date, or which is due to exceptional circumstances. Full information about these special provisions and all provisions as to overcrowding can be obtained free on application to the Local Authority whose address is printed on this card.

1946-47.

County Borough of Newport.

TENANT'S RENT CARD.

Mr. *G. N. Dobbs*

Bungalow

No. *70. Treberth Estate*

Commencement of Tenancy } *3/12/46*

Rates and Water Charges payable by Corporation.

Half-year ending	£	s.	d.
30th September			
31st March		5	9 5

Other Items in Inclusive Rent.

..................................per week ....s..........d.

Corporation Housing Estate Manager:
ALEXANDER H. DUNN,

Collector: **W. BROOKS,**

Housing Bureau, Corn Street.

Medical Officer of Health:
County Borough of Newport—

Dr. H. W. CATTO,
Health Department,
Royal Chambers, High Street,
NEWPORT.

All Receipts for Rent are to be entered on this Card at time of making payment.

DO NOT FOLD.

GEORGE BELL LTD., PRINTERS, NEWPORT.

common, as well as identical homes, appear to have formed strong community bonds that have rarely been matched in Britain. In many cases residents found that their house keys fitted the locks of all the homes on their estate, but few bothered to complain. Crime rates were low, and children played together and freely on the virtually car-less roads.

> My parents loved living there because the children had so much freedom. All the residents had children, and it had a good community spirit. /June Sowerby

At some point most people found themselves looking after other people's children, but few seem to have minded. The low fences meant that everyone knew each other's business, and the postman could vault over them to shorten his journey. Prefab living necessitated participation in community life, and there was little place for secrecy.

> My parents moved into their prefab in 1948. Why I took another three years to arrive I'm not sure. Some of the neighbours had children and called my mother 'the career girl'. I think I surprised a lot of people when I arrived in 1951. My mother eventually told the biggest gossip in the prefabs that she was pregnant, and then watched to see how long she could keep the news to herself before she went to tell another neighbour [there were no telephones]. Sure enough, after just 10 minutes, she ran to another prefab. /Mary Sprakes

90/ Rent card from 1946–47. The small print reveals that the prefab could house up to five people. A child under ten years old counted as 'half' a person, and babies didn't count at all.

 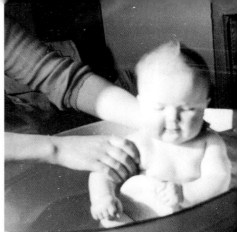

91/ 92/

Many people formed close bonds with their neighbours, something that was no doubt encouraged by the sense of shared experience that they felt.

> Each pair of prefabs shared one water pipe coming into the two homes, and it was possible to call the next-door neighbour by simply running the cold tap in the kitchen and making it rattle. My Mum had her own code to talk to her friend next door. Turning the tap on twice meant 'Come round for a cuppa!', and three would be 'I'm coming round, put the kettle on!' /Ken Wakefield

Most residents considered their prefab 'village' to be superior to the average council estate; it was a special place, and one that was jealously protected. There was even a certain amount of snobbishness directed towards non-prefab residents. Almost as if the residents were part of some great social experiment, they formed their identity from the homes that they lived in – and the bonds

93/

formed were so strong that often several generations of the same family have remained faithful to prefab homes. On some estates each street had a residents association and a penny a week was collected from everyone to fund it.

Most prefabs were home to a nuclear family, with the man typically being the breadwinner. His wife remained at home, often caring for small children. Employment varied, but it was often factory-based.

91/ David Page, aged 6 months, in an Arcon kitchen, 1960. The Treberth estate was connected to the gas mains, so the cooker in the background was gas powered, as was the refrigerator. 92/ Bathing Catherine Dobbs in 1953. Although there was a fitted bath it was easier, and warmer, to bathe babies in a traditional tin bath in front of the fire. 93/ In the summer months toddlers could use the tin bath as a paddling pool. This estate of Arcons in Barking, Essex is long gone, but several Newport Arcons retain a tin bath in their Anderson shelter sheds.

> My father was a part-time fireman and we had a great big fire bell above the bedrooms. If there was a fire the alarm would go off. It shook the house, and dad rushed to the fire station on his bike which was at the ready in the shed. /Mrs J Munday, who grew up in a prefab in Princes Risborough

When the children started going to school (and sometimes before) the woman would often take on some work. Rent varied between estates, but was approximately 14/2d per week in 1946, inclusive of rates. American imported prefabs were slightly cheaper, reflecting their smaller size. The contemporary wage of a typical prefab family was approximately £3 a week. Coal would be delivered twice or even three times a week to enable people to make small purchases, but each family could only buy 3 cwt (about 150 kg) a month because of the rationing that remained in force until 1958. Others were less well catered for:

> We had to collect the coal from the local Gas Works Holders, usually in prams as no one had cars. We were lucky, we had a motorbike and sidecar, but the petrol was only for my husband to get to work with. /Mrs Margaret Parrett, recalling her days in her Solihull Arcon Mk V

The communities often formed regular habits. Monday was washday.

> Beneath the draining board there was a large copper boiler (Mum actually kept the bread in there, for some reason). On washdays she would pull this out, take

94/ Twenty years after the estate was erected this Birmingham Aluminium Bungalow was still providing comfortable accommodation for young families.

95/ 96/

out the bread, clean out the crumbs and fill it with water, light the gas ring and wait. Water was transferred to the dolly tub for 'ponching' the dirty clothes and refilled so that white clothes could be boiled with a 'blue-bag'. All clothes were lifted into a sink full of cold water using large wooden tongues. After rinsing they were mangled (usually by us, if we were there) and hung out to dry … It was a matter of pride to be the first to have a billowing line of washing. Anyone who washed on another day, according to my mother, was a slut [slut meant 'slattern' in the 1940s]. My mum was very house-proud and would invariably take great satisfaction in looking down the gardens to see that she was invariably one of the first to achieve this aim. /Jill Shilvock

Despite the many advantages of prefab living, not everything was idyllic. In particular, many found the insulation of the prefabs inadequate, and poorly fitting windows and doors exacerbated the problem. For some their abiding

97/ 98/

95/ Ken Wakefield in the back garden of his Aluminium Bungalow in Southampton, 1957. 'We could go out to play in the mornings and not return home until teatime, and our parents knew we were OK with our friends.' 96/ Brian Wakefield in the front garden of his Aluminium Bungalow in Southampton, 1961. 97/ Mary Adder and pram outside her Aluminium Bungalow in Hull, 1955. Despite the fact that Tarran prefabs were manufactured in this town, Aluminium Bungalows (which were largely manufactured in the south-west) were erected as part of the Temporary Housing Programme. 98/ This girl on an estate of Arcons at Ripple Road in Barking, Essex, would have enjoyed the freedom of the estate. Few people had cars, and the footpaths between prefabs were a safe network for cycling children.

memory of the prefab was how cold it was in winter. The ducting that was supposed to pipe hot air from the fire to the bedrooms was ineffective, and with little roof-space insulation the heat that was created soon disappeared into the atmosphere. Most people would have been used to bedrooms without heating, but prefabs were especially chilly. Problems with condensation and damp added to the discomfort.

> They were very cold and damp in the winter. I remember standing around a 'Valor' gas heater, freezing, as I waited for my father to come home and light it. I had trouble with my chest due to dampness, which ended as soon as we left the prefab. /Jean Connell

The winter of 1946–47 was one of the worst on record, and one that few prefab dwellers have forgotten. Several still recall the dates of the snows of 27–31 January 1947, which were the heaviest they have ever experienced. Snowdrifts some 6 metres high brought the movement of coal to a standstill, and thousands of homes were without heat and light. The serious shortage of fuel brought Britain to its economic knees. The power cuts caused some four million workers to be laid off, and the freezing temperatures lasted for weeks.

> It was so cold in the winter of 1947 that it froze the goldfish in the bowl, in one night, poor fish. My wife really did cry. They were nice places, but very cold.
> /Mr R H Clements

99/ A group of girls on the Honicknowle estate of Aluminium Bungalows in Plymouth c. 1952.

100/ 101/ 102/

100/ Mary Adder in the kitchen of her Aluminium Bungalow with her favourite doll, Nina, in 1959. The internal window between the kitchen and lounge is just visible. 101/ Mary Adder and friends sledging outside her Aluminium Bungalow in Hull in the late 1950s. The children would happily move from estate to estate in search of things to do, and two of the girls pictured lived on a neighbouring estate where the houses were of standard construction. 102/ Mary Adder and her best friend, Carole Crawforth in the garden of her Aluminium Bungalow. 'I had no idea that I lived in a glorified shack when I was little, because lots of us did.' 103/ Children playing with their dog in the garden of their Aluminium Bungalow on the Brynmenyn estate in South Wales. The large TV aerial needed to pick up both the channels available is just visible to the right of the boy's head.

103/

That winter the milk, bread and coal had to be delivered on horse-drawn sledges. Many families began to use electric fires and eventually the inevitable happened. The overloaded wiring buried in the walls became overheated, and in one instance burst into flames. This particular home was quickly reduced to ashes, not even the framework remained. /Alan Crowe, recalling how the US-imported prefabs were not designed for UK winters

Clothing

Most people expected that when the war ended, so would the despised rationing system. However, Britain had run up huge wartime debts, and rationing continued under Clement Attlee's 'austerity measures'.

Men who had served six months or more in the services were issued with a set of civilian clothes; two million were kitted out in 'demob' (demobilisation) suits. Each man was given a choice of suit, and issued with a raincoat, a shirt

104/   105/

with two collars, a hat, a tie, shoes and two pairs of socks. Rationing continued for clothing, and in September 1945 the ration was cut to just 36 coupons per adult per year (it had been 66 coupons during the war).

The list below illustrates the number of coupons needed to buy a range of garments:

woman's nightdress = 6 coupons
man's overcoat = 16 coupons

104/ The Sandfields estate of Aluminium Bungalows at Port Talbot was ideal for children as the recreation area was one of the largest beaches in South Wales. 105/ A bicycle as a Christmas present meant freedom for Ruth Haynes' daughter, pictured here c. 1952. 106/ Mary Adder proudly displaying the must-have Christmas present of 1961, a pogo stick.

106/

dress = 11 coupons
underpants = 4 coupons
handkerchief = 1/2 coupon
pyjamas = 8 coupons.

People were expected to 'Make do and Mend', repairing clothes and making new clothes out of old.[1] This sometimes involved unravelling old knitwear in order to recycle the wool into new garments. Curtains and tablecloths were cut up to make skirts and dresses, and in some cases women even drew black lines down the back of their legs with make-up, to give the impression that they were wearing nylon stockings. For those who didn't mind buying from the black market, 'spivs' could provide most luxury items (such as nylons) at a price.

Utility-brand clothing had been introduced in 1941, identifying the standardised clothes which were endorsed by the government. The brand dictated the materials used in clothing manufacture. For example, a gentleman's suit was allowed to have a maximum of three pockets, no turn-ups, and a maximum of three buttons. Women's clothing was not allowed to have elastic waistbands or 'fancy belts', and shoe heels were restricted to a maximum height of 5 centimetres.

Princess (now Queen) Elizabeth's wedding in 1947 was an opportunity for women to get out their glad-rags and celebrate the beginning of the easing of clothing restrictions. The last clothing coupons were issued in September 1948, and the Utility scheme for clothing was finally wound up in 1952.

Food

Groceries would typically be delivered to the prefab estate on a daily basis. Some shops were located in disused Nissen huts. Often the (daily) milkman would pour the milk straight into the jugs of the owner, and he also brought chocolate milk drinks called 'Mickey's' that were a treat for the children.

> Mr Lister brought our weekly shopping order for all the time we lived there (1948–62). We had good meals and a box of 'Weekend' chocolates every Friday. Mum rode her bike to the shop for her veg, and Mr Bottrill brought the meat. The rent man was called Mr Halt. He was a pleasant old chap and often had a cup of tea and confided with my mum which of the neighbours were in arrears with the rent. /Mary Sprakes

Wartime rationing had restricted the range and quantity of foods that people could buy, but had probably also provided most with their first experience of an adequate diet. People ate little fat, sugar and meat, but plenty of vegetables and home-grown fruits. During the war infant mortality rates fell dramatically, as did a number of diseases that are related to dietary deficiencies. Ration books enabled people to keep track of their goods. The books were full of coupons which were cut out and used to buy a fixed amount of rationed foods each week. The weekly adult ration varied slightly from month to month according to availability, but typically included:

3 pints of milk
Meat to the value of 1s 2d (rations varied monthly; this represents an average)
1 egg (or 1 packet of dried eggs every two months)
3–4 oz cheese
4 oz bacon and ham
2 oz tea
8 oz sugar
2 oz butter
2 oz cooking fat
+ 16 points a month for other rationed foods (usually tinned) subject to availability. 16 points would, for example, buy 1 tin of fish, 2 lb of dried fruit or 8 lb of split peas.

These restrictions were maintained in the post-war period, and in 1947 bread and potatoes were rationed for the first time. Cereal, offal, fruit and vegetables remained unrationed where they could be obtained. Milk was often in short supply because so much pasture had been ploughed up during the war.

Each prefab had been provided with a large garden plot, providing ample room for residents to grow their own fruit and vegetables. Rationing restricted

107/ Facsimile of a Ministry of Food ration book. It wasn't until 1954 that butter and meat were taken off ration.

PAGE 8

FILL IN THE OTHER SIDE OF THIS COUNTERFOIL
FOR YOUR RETAILER TO DETACH

The Retailer's name must also be written on page 2.

E SPARE 32 / 32 SPARE E	E SPARE 38 / 38 SPARE E	E SPARE 44 / 44 SPARE E	DO NOT FORGET TO FILL IN YOUR RETAILERS' NAMES ON PAGE 2.	
E SPARE 31 / 31 SPARE E	E SPARE 37 / 37 SPARE E	E SPARE 43 / 43 SPARE E		
E SPARE 30 / 30 SPARE E	E SPARE 36 / 36 SPARE E	E SPARE 42 / 42 SPARE E	E SPARE 48 / 48 SPARE E	E SPARE 52 / 52 SPARE E
E SPARE 29 / 29 SPARE E	E SPARE 35 / 35 SPARE E	E SPARE 41 / 41 SPARE E	E SPARE 47 / 47 SPARE E	E SPARE 51 / 51 SPARE E
E SPARE 28 / 28 SPARE E	E SPARE 34 / 34 SPARE E	E SPARE 40 / 40 SPARE E	E SPARE 46 / 46 SPARE E	E SPARE 50 / 50 SPARE E
E SPARE 27 / 27 SPARE E	E SPARE 33 / 33 SPARE E	E SPARE 39 / 39 SPARE E	E SPARE 45 / 45 SPARE E	E SPARE 49 / 49 SPARE E

MONTHLY A COUNTERFOIL—R.B.9

Holder's Name ....
(BLOCK LETTERS)
Address ....
(BLOCK LETTERS)

Name and Address of Retailer ....

RATION BOOK SERIAL NUMBER

NATIONAL REGISTRATION NUMBER

MONTHLY "A" JUNE	MONTHLY "A" APRIL	MONTHLY "A" FEB	MONTHLY "A" DEC	MONTHLY "A" OCT	MONTHLY "A" AUG
MONTHLY "A" MAY	MONTHLY "A" MARCH	MONTHLY "A" JAN	MONTHLY "A" NOV	MONTHLY "A" SEPT	MONTHLY "A" JULY

July 42

MONTHLY "B" JUNE	MONTHLY "B" APRIL	MONTHLY "B" FEB	MONTHLY "B" DEC	MONTHLY "B" OCT	MONTHLY "B" AUG
MONTHLY "B" MAY	MONTHLY "B" MARCH	MONTHLY "B" JAN	MONTHLY "B" NOV	MONTHLY "B" SEPT	MONTHLY "B" JULY

MONTHLY B COUNTERFOIL—R.B.9

Holder's Name ....
(BLOCK LETTERS)
Address ....
(BLOCK LETTERS)

Name and Address of Retailer ....

RATION BOOK SERIAL NUMBER

NATIONAL REGISTRATION NUMBER

bananas to children less than 12 years old, and many grew their own fruit including apples, raspberries, loganberries, strawberries, gooseberries and blackcurrants.

> There were so many people growing strawberries here at one point that we had a competition to see who could grow the largest fruit. After that people used to call our street 'Strawberry Lane'. /Alan Page, Treberth Arcon estate at Newport

People behaved like squirrels, bottling preserves at every opportunity in case supplies ran out. Some residents used the copper wash boiler to help them produce bottled preserves of plums, apples and even runner beans.

108/ Irene Ottoway making a cup of Horlicks in a US-imported prefab, Willesden in the mid 1950s. Note the budgerigar cage in the background.

> I used to grow lots of vegetables, especially Webb's Wonderful lettuce, which would just about fit on the top of a bucket as the soil was so good. /Prefab resident Henry Dodwell, who won several 'Garden of the Year' awards from his local council

Meat was considered to be a treat during the days of rationing, and housewives would look for opportunities to make their limited supplies stretch as far as possible.[2] Residents would trap rabbits to supplement their diet. A rabbit hung from the key in the kitchen door was at the perfect height for skinning.

> We used to eat a lot stews. If it was 'meat and two veg' then dad had most of the meat, and us kids would get a sausage. /Alan Page

Left-over food would be recycled into rissoles or 'bubble and squeak', and even the scraps would find a home when the 'pig-swill lady' called in to collect scraps for her pigs. People would have been conscious of wartime propaganda from the Ministry of Food that boasted that housewives saving scraps saved the Empire:

> Because of the pail, the scraps were saved,
> Because of the scraps, the pigs were saved,
> Because of the pigs, the rations were saved,
> Because of the rations, the ships were saved,
> Because of the ships, the island was saved,
> Because of the island, the Empire was saved,
> And all because of the housewife's pail.

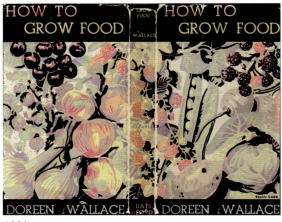

109/

The Minister of Food, Lord Woolton, gave his name to recipes such as Woolton [vegetable] Pie, as well as offering novel food suggestions such as whale meat which was newly available just after the war. Cooks were advised that the odd flavour could be subdued by overnight soaking in vinegar! Woolton was remarkably popular with the public, aided by cartoons of 'Dr Carrot' and 'Potato Pete', and 'Food Flashes' in the cinema. The Minister ensured that children received daily milk, cod-liver oil and orange juice via welfare clinics or school, and free school meals were introduced for children from poorer families.

109/ The distinctive Brian Cook dustjacket to *How to Grow Food* by Doreen Wallace, one of a series of 'Home-Front Handbooks' published by Batsford to help people adapt to wartime and post-war life. 110/ Labelled enamel storage canisters such as these became ubiquitous, and the bottling of pickles and preserves was common.

palaces for the people/

> I was a pupil at Henry Gotch Infants School, Kettering, where children received one teaspoon of cod-liver oil, followed by a much more palatable teaspoon of concentrated orange juice. We queued for this ritual every school-day morning, each dose administered from the same spoon and without the spoon being cleaned between recipients. Milk monitors (children from the top class) distributed the milk during the afternoon. /Andrew Wood

Marguerite Patten was employed by the Ministry of Food to devise new recipes that made best use of available ingredients, and to publicise them through demonstrations, leaflets and radio broadcasts. Recipes encouraged housewives to try new foodstuffs such as fresh-salted cod (that required soaking), rissoles made without beef, cakes without sugar and tea without tea leaves! Apart from novel recipe ideas, the Ministry also came up with interesting gift ideas such as the 'hot packed-lunch box' that was a disused gas-mask carrier filled with hay.

Mock Duck (courtesy Marguerite Patten)
Cooking time: 45 minutes
Quantity: four helpings

1 lb sausagemeat
8 oz cooking apples, peeled and grated
8 oz onions, grated
1 teaspoon chopped sage or ½ teaspoon dried sage

METHOD: Spread half the sausagemeat into a flat layer in a well-greased baking tin or shallow casserole. Top with the apples, onions and sage. Add the rest of the sausagemeat and shape this top layer to look as much like a duck as possible. Cover with well-greased paper and bake in the centre of a moderately hot oven.

Ration restrictions ultimately meant that most people were better fed than they had been in the 1930s, and of the prefab residents interviewed most claimed that although rationing was inconvenient, it wasn't 'that bad' in practice. The restrictions forced the prefab generation to use their ingenuity when it came to using food resources, and hundreds of new and varied recipes appeared. Housewives gladly swapped the results of their recipe experiments.

The Prefab Garden

Each prefab had a large garden for growing the fruit and vegetables that proved so important in supplementing the diet of residents. In some cases tenants rented allotments to further increase their food production. Government propaganda and the successful wartime 'Dig for Victory' campaign would have been fresh in people's minds.

> We want not only the big man with the plough but the little man with the spade to get busy this autumn ... Let 'Dig for Victory' be the motto of everyone with a garden. /Broadcast by Rob Hudson, Minister for Agriculture, in October 1939

The government knew that approximately a quarter of Britain's vegetables could be grown by individuals on their small garden plots, and the wartime posters that implied that you were helping the country if you were self-suffi-

111/ 112/

cient continued in the late 1940s. By 1945 three-quarters of the food consumed in Britain was produced in Britain. Lawns had been dug up for potatoes, cabbages, carrots and beans. Public parks were given over to arable production, and roadside verges, railway embankments, golf courses and even house roofs had been put to work in producing vegetables for the home market. Some prefab residents were not content with growing fruit and vegetables, and introduced poultry and rabbits to supplement their diet.

111/ Mr Tom Crow planting a rockery in front of his US-imported prefab. 112/ Even though much of the garden of this Arcon in Cardiff was given over to vegetable production, there was still room for decorative borders of flowers. 113/ The garden of this Universal prefab won Best Garden in the Borough in 1955. The trophy was a source of great pride for the owner. 114/ Lily Hudson proudly displaying the roses in the garden of her Phoenix prefab garden at Podsmead, Gloucester.

113/

114/

Many prefab tenants would have been enjoying having their own garden for the first time. In many cases they would take possession of the prefab with just an expanse of mud for a garden. Some South Wales estates were built on slag heaps, so the men would head out to the mountains with wheelbarrows to bring topsoil painstakingly back to their gardens.

By the early 1950s many found that they could give part of their gardens over to a play area for their children and decorative planting. Flowering plants such as roses, and summer bedding plants such as begonias, lobelia and alyssum, were all popular. Simply having lawns and flowering borders was itself a social statement, as the poor had to use any land available as a kitchen garden.

Gardening became a very popular pursuit, with some residents devoting all their leisure daylight hours to them. Estates organised annual garden competitions, and often prefab residents would win the local-authority competitions

115/ Hanging out the washing to dry in the garden of a US-imported prefab in Willesden, London. An Anderson shelter is serving as a garden shed; they were often used to store coal. 116/ Jill Shilvock and friends in the garden of her Phoenix prefab at Podsmead. 'We felt that we were part of something new and exciting. The estate absolutely swarmed with young kids, and the joy that we got from all those open fields, streams and "real" adventure playgrounds is something I will never forget.' 117/ Margaret McCall and Sandra Roberts outside Margaret's Aluminium Bungalow in 1954. Note the rustic trellis made from wood taken from hedgerows.

116/ 117/

that were open to all. Gardening societies flourished as homeowners grew vegetables and fruit as well as flowers and lawns.

> One of the very best features of the prefabs was the large garden that went with them. My father, a Pool of London dockworker, was a very keen gardener who grew vegetables, flowers and fruit trees. He also built a summerhouse, a greenhouse, garden swings, a hammock and a seesaw. During the coronation year he followed the trend and planted our front garden in red, white and blue flowers. /Margaret Sinnott, recalling her prefab days in Hackney Wick 1945–1959

The vegetable plots in front gardens which were converted into display areas invariably included a small patch of lawn with tidy flowering borders (often tea roses), visible through the wire-mesh fences. Gnomes were popular additions to such scenes, as were concrete wishing wells and other fantasy features.

118/   119/

Country living

For some, prefab living was not dissimilar to how they imagined rural cottage life. Residents would sometimes help out on adjoining farms in exchange for fresh eggs, a real treat in days of rationing.

> We had a wonderful life there with spectacular views of farmland. The resident farm peacock used to come into our garden and display to our hens; its fan would cover the whole window. /Elizabeth Clancy recalls life in a Lichfield prefab

Prefab estates often gained a reputation for being better places to live than other local-authority accommodation. Crime was low, and resident satisfaction

118/ All-electric Ecko wireless c. 1945. The radio was the most popular source of home entertainment. 119/ 'War-Time Civilian wireless receiver', 1944.

was unusually high. One night someone added the sign 'You are now entering Sleepy Valley' to one of the lampposts on the Sturminster Estate in Bristol – there wasn't a sound after 6 o'clock.

Many urban dwellers were discovering the countryside for the first time in post-war Britain, partly because they had moved out to suburban areas, but also because people were generally more mobile than they had been previously. To address this, Batsford launched a series of 'Home–Front Handbooks' designed to 'meet the needs of those who, through wartime circumstances, must seek their own entertainment instead of finding it readymade and to hand'. Harry Batsford himself wrote the popular *How to See the Country* (1940, reprinted 1946), and other volumes included the useful *How to Grow Food* by Doreen Wallace. Topographical writing was experiencing a revival, most notably with the popular 'Face of Britain' county guidebook series. These books provided the consumable image of romantic escape for the weekend trip, a way for people to consume the English landscape as a romantic commodity. In these and other topographical guidebooks the rural landscape was painted as a haven from urban life, and the opposite of all things bad about cramped living in the towns.

For many people the move out to prefab estates that bordered open farmland was a move towards a rural future and away from the slums and war-torn town and city centres. It isn't surprising that being allocated a country 'cottage' with a large garden and acres of space in which the children could play was an idyllic scenario that many urbanites envied.

> Sometimes if Mum was in a good mood she would let us have an old nylon stocking and from this we would make a fishing net. We found conkers each year,

120/ 121/

and followed the seasons of marbles, jacks, skipping, "stills" using lollipop sticks, cat's cradles etc. We made bows and arrows, and catapults and go-karts. Everything we did cost practically nothing, which is was a good thing as we didn't have any money. It sounds idyllic, and it was. /Jill Shilvock recalling her Gloucestershire prefab childhood

120/ Christine Valente outside her Birmingham Arcon in her new Girl Guides uniform, 1953. The Coronation poster behind her was no doubt taken from a magazine or newspaper. 121/ The street party for the Coronation on the Treberth estate in Newport, 1953. Many of the individuals pictured still lived on the estate in 2002. 122/ In fancy dress for a Coronation party on a Birmingham prefab estate. 123, 124/ pages 174–175: A selection of games and toys displayed in the reconstructed Aluminium Bungalow at the Museum of Welsh Life.

122/

Leisure

Much leisure time was spent in the prefab, and the 'wireless' (radio) was the centre of home entertainment, offering a wide range of programmes. Typically it included news, drama, sport, religion, music (light to classical), and 'variety' or light entertainment. The *Radio Times* sold millions of copies every week. *Woman's Hour* was first broadcast in 1946 (at 2 pm), and *Children's Hour* with Uncle Mac (Derek McCulloch) was consistently and enormously popular. Not only did the wireless cater for different social needs (education, information, and entertainment), it also provided programmes for different sectional interests within the listening public (children, women, businessmen, farmers, fishermen, etc.). The wireless brought the wider world into the prefab living room, kept people aware of food prices and availability, and provided housewives with cooking tips.

  The most popular show on the wireless was *ITMA* (*It's That Man Again*),

123, 124/

starring Tommy Handley, which had entertained audiences with its satirical comedy throughout the war. With hostilities over, the comedy introduced a new cast and settings, and continued to attract huge audiences until it ended in January 1949. At one point it was estimated that most of Britain came to a standstill at 8.30 every Thursday night to hear of Tommy's antics. So popular was Handley that when he died of a brain haemorrhage just days after the final show, the streets were lined with mourners for his funeral procession, and he was given the honour of a memorial service at St Paul's Cathedral. Other new post-war series included *Dick Barton–Special Agent*, which guaranteed a cliffhanger ending every week, and the soap opera *Mrs Dale's Diary*.

Few prefab residents would have noticed that television began broadcasting again in June 1946, as the sets were prohibitively expensive. Had they had a set they could have watched coverage of the Olympic Games that was hosted in Britain in 1948, the first since the Berlin Olympics of 1936. In 1951 the Festival of Britain set up on the South Bank of the Thames in London, showcasing the best of British goods. People flocked to London to see the Skylon, a futuristic obelisk, and the Dome of Discovery. Many returned to their prefab estates with souvenirs branded with the logo designed by Sir Basil Spence. It wasn't really until the coronation in 1953 that television started to threaten radio as the primary source of home entertainment. Those prefabs that did have televisions in the early 1950s had to have large H shaped aerials in the garden that usually required a tall pole with stays to support it.

125/ If you could afford a holiday in the late 1940s or 1950s, it could well have been to a prefab of another sort, such as these timber-framed holiday chalets.

127/

We only had BBC at the prefab because of the aerial on the house. To get ITV we had to have a mast in the garden and Dad couldn't be bothered. /Mary Sprakes

Post-war cinema provided an escape from austerity, and Hollywood films filled with excitement and romance were watched by millions every week. Before the main film was screened viewers would be shown a short newsreel that kept them informed of the reconstruction effort, and several Pathé News reels were shown of 'amazing, flat-packed' prefabs. Cinemagoers in 1945 would have seen 'Mrs Churchill Inspects Prefab Home' and 'American Houses Being Erected Across the Country', and others followed the factory production and

126/ Cover of the souvenir programme for the 1951 Festival of Britain. 127/ Mary Adder and her mother on their annual holiday in Bridlington. They travelled by train from their Aluminium Bungalow in Hull.

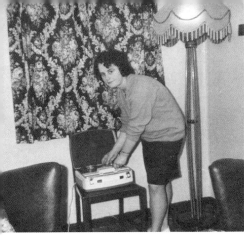 

128/ 129/

export of prefabs to Northern Ireland. These reels not only reflect public interest in the subject, but also illustrate the government's publicity machine at work.

DIY became popular for prefab dwellers, encouraged by the need to make furnishings for the home. Knitting, crochet, and the production of rag rugs were all widely practised, and not only by women.

> Both Dad and myself were interested in photography and we often used to black

128/ Margaret McCall playing the 'Tapemaster' machine in the lounge of her Aluminium Bungalow in 1959. 129/ Margaret McCall and friend Sheila dancing in the smaller bedroom of her Aluminium Bungalow in 1959. 130/ Margaret McCall and parents in the lounge of their Aluminium Bungalow in 1960. Margaret had just left school, aged 15.

130/

out our small kitchen with blankets from the beds to do our own developing and printing. It was mainly black and white in those days, so on my eleventh birthday dad bought me a hand-colouring kit and I immediately set out to colour all our old prints. /Alan Crowe, who grew up in an imported US prefab (see page 90)

Few prefab residents would have owned cars in the 1940s, and shortages of petrol meant there were few vehicles on the road and a great reliance on public transport, which was also restricted.

Mostly we played on the concrete roads, there were no cars to speak of. We knew one person who had a car, but he lived three streets away /Maddy Prior, recalling life on an estate of Aluminium Bungalows in Layton, Blackpool

Several prefab estates clubbed together to fund youth clubs and social events

131/

that were held in nearby buildings. These might have been church halls, community halls, or, as was the case at the Bishpool Arcon estate in Newport, the former munitions factory.

> There was a park for the children, and there was never any trouble. We went to Christchurch every Sunday, and dancing once or twice a week in St Teilo's church in town. It was the 'Old Time' dances, I used to love them. In general it was just the men that went to the pubs. /Minnie Louvain Owen, Treberth estate, Newport

> The prefabs were a wonderful environment for children to grow up in; we had the freedom to do more or less what we liked within reason. We could go out to play in the mornings and not return home until teatime, and our parents knew we were OK with our friends. We had fun places to go like the dump or tip in Elgar Road, or the old brickworks in Butts Road. Life was good for kids in those days.

132/ 133/

It's a shame that children today cannot be given the freedom we enjoyed.
/Ken Wakefield

In the larger towns and cities such as Bristol and Newport with numerous prefab estates the residents would organise cricket and football competitions between estates. Sundays might include a visit to the local church. Occasionally even these were temporary buildings constructed like Nissen huts with squared-off ends. Children might be sent to youth clubs, the cubs, scouts or the Boys Brigade. However, for the most part they would have made their own entertainment either on or off the prefab estate.

131/ Diane Page in her best dress outside her Arcon in Newport in 1961. 132/ Sharon and Christine Page are also dressed up, no doubt for a wedding. 133/ Mary Valente with daughters Pauline and Christine outside their Birmingham Arcon c. 1959.

134/ By 1961 this young man who lived in an Essex Uni-Seco could afford a motorcycle. Note the original prefab shed behind him.

> Some of my toys were battery-powered. They had been bought for me in America by an uncle who worked on the Cunard liners. The problem with batteries is they went flat and useless after a very short time. I had seen Dad partly recharge them by wedging the coal shovel into the front of the fire and placing the battery on to it for the heat to charge it up. If Dad could do it I thought there is no problem with me doing it as well. I placed the battery in front of the fire but figured it would charge quicker if I forgot about the shovel and put it on the bars keeping the coke in. I forgot about it and the next thing the battery was spread across the ceiling!
> /Ken Wakefield

Holidays

The traditional summer holiday disappeared for all but the rich during world War 2, and those that did get time off from work were encouraged to take holidays at home. It isn't surprising then that when the barbed wire and notices of mines were cleared from the beaches of the south and east coast, those who could afford it took holidays, even if it was just a daytrip.

> I remember our holidays in the '40s and '50s with great affection. I was the youngest of ten, and was the only one left at home in the prefab with mum and dad. We used to have a week away each year. Mostly we holidayed at Ramsgate in Kent. It was during the time when the Americans were based at Manston Aerodrome. Ramsgate was full of them. All in dress uniforms, and looking very smart indeed! They were very well mannered, without exception, and were great fun to have around. /Terry Wade

Although the majority couldn't afford a holiday of any sort in the late 1940s, many prefab dwellers found they could manage occasional day-trips by public transport, or even a few days away.

> We had three holidays during my childhood. The first was staying at a cottage at a village called Framilode, which by car from where we used to live, I now find, is only 15 minutes away! I went by bicycle. I can remember being on a seat on Dad's crossbar. We got bitten by bed-bugs/fleas. Our second holiday was to a caravan park in Exmouth. There was a loudspeaker on the corners of the site which blared out music. I particularly remember one tune – I think it is called 'The British Grenadiers' … The site had nothing on it, neither did the sands and the toilet on the beach was so disgusting you had to be really desperate to go in there. For our third holiday we had a proper holiday at St Ives, Cornwall, in a guest-house owned by a childhood friend of my mother from Derby. /Jill Shilvock

Others earned money on working holidays.

> Many families in my area of London (some lived in prefabs, some not) went hop-picking during the summer holidays. A large lorry would pull up and many families would disappear for six weeks to Kent for a working holiday. I would be banished to my Gran's in Essex for two months. /Patricia Skeels

It was quite common for people to travel only a few miles for their holiday break, and not always to the obvious resorts. The speed of public transport would have made only ten or 20 miles seem like a considerable distance. In some cases prefab residents would find themselves holidaying in other pre-fabricated homes – the chalets that they rented.

In the summer Mum would take us down to Weston shore with our friends as a day's outing. It seemed as though it took forever to get there, and even longer coming back. Would anyone walk that far now with umpteen screaming kids without a car? I doubt it. And would anyone want to swim there? I doubt that too! /Brian Wakefield

In Newport, prefab residents clubbed together, collecting a weekly amount of 5 shillings that was kept in a pontoon fund to pay for the summer holiday. When the time came for the factories to break (usually a regular fortnight) virtually all the residents from the estate would travel together, chartering a bus to save costs.

135/ Jill Shilvock and friends in the garden of her Phoenix in Podsmead, 1964. Her mother was always the first to get her washing on the line on a Monday.

From 1947 through about 1954, we (Mum, Dad my younger brother and I) left our prefab at Newport for exotic places such as Barry Island, Southerndown, Porthcawl, and our favourite of all was the Gower Peninsular (all within 50 miles). Rain or shine (mostly rain) we went for a week, and usually stayed in a 'chalet' of about 10 feet by 10 feet near Limeslade Bay. As a kid of ten or so, I enjoyed the Mumbles trams and the Mumbles Pier with all its wicked penny slot machines and the pier boards that continually gave us huge splinters in our bare feet, which my Mum had to remove with a needle or hatpin! /John Leonard, who grew up in an Arcon Mk V

The 'bonfire of controls'

In 1949 Harold Wilson, then President of the Board of Trade, announced his 'bonfire of controls' and removed the ration restrictions on 60 commodities. A year later clothes rationing was abolished, and by 1950 the majority of restrictions had been removed. It wasn't until 1954, however, that butter and meat were taken off ration. The need to 'make do' influenced most areas of life, and installed a sense of frugality that has remained with prefab residents to this day. Many of the last few remaining prefab gardens are still partly given over to the production of marrows, tomatoes, potatoes and kidney beans, decades after rationing ended.

[1] See Baker 1991 and Wood 1989 for further reading on post-war fashion.
[2] See Patten 1990 for ration recipes.

permanent prefabs/

> Prefabrication is in its infancy. But it is no sickly bastard – it is a lively child with a good pedigree and a great future and the building industry will be wise to adopt it. If it does not, then other industries with more energy and imagination will do so, and will reap the reward.[1]

The 156,000 prefabs constructed under the Temporary Housing Programme only made a small dent in the massive housing shortage of post-war Britain, and experiments continued into non-traditional house construction.[2] A further 315,000 permanent houses were erected in the period to 1949, some of traditional construction, but many which involved some degree of prefabrication. The Government subsidised the development of these non-traditional systems of housing as well as funding research through the Ministry of Works, and the Department of Scientific and Industrial Research. Thirteen blocks of prototype houses were erected at Northolt in Middlesex in 1943–44 to measure the costs of producing standardised homes.

Dozens of types of non-traditional-construction houses were produced in the decades after World War 2, and most included at least some form of factory prefabrication. System-building, where factory-prefabricated panels were attached to a framework on-site, became increasingly common. Many rapidly erected low-cost blocks of flats were constructed during the 1950s and 1960s using the system-built approach, and were heralded as the solution to the problems of slums and homelessness. Whether such properties are actually

136/ Two-storey Spooner prefab houses at Bortswick in Yorkshire, 1949. The same J L Spooner who produced single-storey prefabs under the THP programme manufactured these timber-framed houses.

'prefabricated' is debatable, but residents of single-storey homes usually refer to their homes with the term 'prefab'.

> What are the advantages of system building? The buildings can be erected more quickly than by using traditional methods and a much smaller labour force is needed on the site. Such buildings are often lighter in weight than conventional buildings and there is a considerable saving in materials and foundation costs. Furthermore, they are often more suitable for the purpose for which they are built, better insulated, with improved systems of heating, ventilation and layout.[3]

Although the new construction techniques explored within the THP had excited architects, many were frustrated that so much money was invested in temporary houses when it could have been used to construct permanent homes. John Gloag and Grey Wornum published *House out of Factory* in 1946 as an evangelical text promoting prefabrication, and encouraging the public to 'consider their verdict' on the many illustrated examples. They attacked the temporary homes that would soon become 'the most repellent types of slum'[4] and promoted the permanent prefab types produced by Orlit, Clothed Concrete Constructions, Howard & Company, the British Iron and Steel Federation, Keyhouse Unibuilt, Braithwaite, Jicwood and the Timber Development Association.

> If enough people would forget their preconceived ideas about architecture and building and make up their minds to live in their own stimulating, convenient and revolutionary century, all the people could have good, cheap, comfortable houses, so easy to run that harassed housewives would not be old women at 40 – they would be young women still.[5]

In practice even the most successful of the post-war permanent prefabs, the BISF and Airey programmes (with some 30,000 and 20,000 homes respectively) proved no cheaper than traditional construction techniques. However, like the THP prefab bungalows, they did address the need for 'instant' factory-produced homes that required little skilled labour for construction. Although building trade unions had been concerned about the effect of prefabrication on their industry, in fact many non-traditional houses actually created employment – scarce supplies of bricks and other building materials limited building jobs in the decade after the war.

137/ Easiform concrete houses erected in Southampton in 1946.

139/

Swedish imported prefabs

Although technically not part of the THP (the houses were categorised as permanent), thousands of Swedish timber prefabs were being imported and erected at the same time as the THP bungalows. These made a sizeable contribution to new housing provision in rural areas, and particularly in Scotland where the Forestry Commission erected them.[6] Britain had been importing Scandinavian prefabs for use as council housing since the 1920s, and the post-war types were modified to better suit the British climate than their pre-war 'Scanhouse' cousins. Single- and two-storey examples were introduced.

Swedish manufacturers IBO of Knivsta, Sesam built the prefabs that Britain

138/ Swedish timber prefabs arrive at Crown Wharf, London, in 1946. 139/ Swedish prefab panels stacked at the Temporary Housing Distribution Centre in Liverpool in 1946.

140/

imported from about 1934.[7] They were of heavy timber panel construction, with outer and inner sheathing of boards, and an infilling of insulation built on a stud frame. The frame was merely to contain the insulation and the panels functioned as solid load-bearing members. These large boards arrived at London docks incorporating door and window openings specially detailed for each house type. The panels were assembled on site with intermediate studs and key pieces. What made the Swedish system unique was that it had been designed for assembly by the unskilled labour of the owner-occupiers (only the flues require special skill). Some 50,000 people in Stockholm alone had erect-

140/ Swedish houses under construction in 1946 at Great Ellingham in Norfolk. Most Swedish prefabs were erected in rural areas such as this, where emergency housing for farm workers was required. 141/ The Swedish houses at Great Ellingham in Norfolk, nearing completion.

142/ Swedish house in Canning Town, east London, 1945. This rare photograph shows the Prisoners of War who erected the building.

ed their own prefab homes before 1939, but in Britain the Swedish houses were erected by the local authorities.

The Government planned to import 10,000 Swedish prefab homes, but it reneged on the deal as Sweden wasn't in the Sterling zone and Britain could not afford to pay for them with dollars. In the end only 2444 made it to our shores, and the best surviving group is now just outside Doncaster. Surviving examples tend to be in eastern England where it is drier and the timber has lasted better.

BL8 Aluminium Bungalows

After the end of production of the THP AIROH Aluminium Bungalows, the factories that had produced them started making permanent versions. The most common semi-detached variety was labelled the BL8 by the Bristol Aircraft Company. Those sold by Hawksley Constructions Ltd retailed as Hawksley Bungalows, and were available in detached and semi-detached forms, although it appears that most local authorities bought the semi-detached versions.

The BL8s were fabricated in four sections and assembled on a concrete plinth. The outside skin and roof was made of aircraft 'Duralamin' (aluminium alloy). The traditional brick chimneystacks were built up in sections on the ground and hoisted into position by crane. Fitted with galvanised steel windows, a 'Claco' fireplace, highly polished thermoplastic floor coverings, and an induction fan to distribute warm air around the building, the BL8s were generally of an improved design. Residents were encouraged to turn the fan on an hour before retiring to bed to ensure a warm bedroom. Hangers could be suspended from the timber cornices in every room.

The design of the BL8 proved popular, and a number were exported to

143/

Australia to be used by workers on the Snowy Mountain hydroelectric scheme. Demonstrating their portability, these were then moved a second time (to the Woomera rocket range) and have since been relocated a third time.

The production of BL8s appears to have ended in 1953 when the factories returned to major aircraft projects. However, estates in good condition can still be seen in Redditch and Edinburgh, and there are still several in Northern Ireland. The Edinburgh examples at Moredun are even served by an aluminium prefab school (Fernieside) which was also manufactured by the Bristol Aircraft Company.

London County Council Mobiles

Known as 'LCC Mobiles' and erected between 1963 and 1967, the London County Council prefabs came 15 years later than the majority of single-storey British post-war prefabs but make an interesting comparison in that they were

144/

143/ BL8s at Dolphin Road in Redditch, photographed in the 1950s. 144/ Semi-detached version of the BL8 Aluminium Bungalow at the Crapen, Cam in Gloucestershire. 145/ pages 202–203: BL8s at Dolphin Road in Redditch erected in 1948. Residents have successfully fought to prevent their demolition.

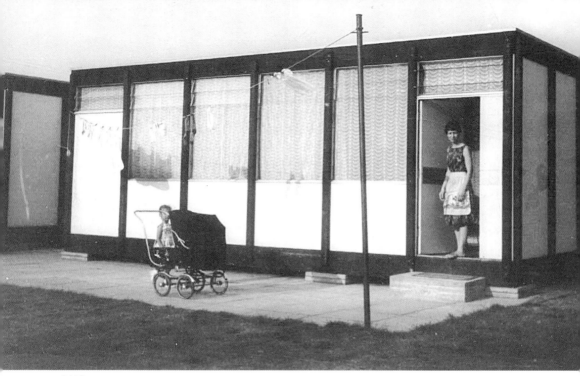

146/

146/ Doreen Bregula at the door of her London County Council mobile home prefab at Essian Street in Stepney, 1964. 147/ Karen Bregula and friend outside her LCC prefab in 1969. Note how the neighbouring prefab (left) had been boarded up by this time.

147/

highly prefabricated. Designed by Hubert Bennett (LCC chief architect) and six assistants, the LCCs were made to last 20 years by Calders of Co. Durham. They cost just £1239 each.[8] Calders also manufactured a two-storey prefab using the same construction system. It featured external walls of white laminated asbestos with a dark-stained cedar trim. The flat roof of the LCC gave it a particularly modern, boxy appearance.

    Each prefab was joined in the middle on the side elevation. The rear half contained the main bedroom and the living room (with back door), and the front contained the second bedroom, hall, bathroom, cupboard and kitchen. All this was within a 24-by-17-foot (7.3- by 5.2-metre) rectangle, making the LCCs considerably smaller than the THP bungalows. Three-bedroom models were available, with the extra room sticking out awkwardly from the rear as a modular unit.

    Internally, the floors were covered in Polyvinyl and warmth was provided by

148/

149/

a 'Halcyon Heater' in the living room, with louvres to distribute the heat to the bedrooms.

The LCC prefabs were often erected in small numbers on bomb-damaged sites that remained unreconstructed two decades after the end of the war. In some instances they were replacements for the 1944 THP prefabs that had started to decay. Many small groups of LCCs were introduced in east and south-east London, with small estates in Plumstead, New Cross, Blackfriars, and Elephant & Castle all surviving into the 1990s. One group of them at Salmon Lane, Limehouse (E14) became known as the home of a community of writers, painters and designers.

British Iron and Steel Federation Houses

The most successful of the two-storey prefabs were undoubtedly the British Iron and Steel Federation houses (BISFs). Dating back to government experi-

150/

ments in 1943 at Northolt, and much publicised in contemporary literature, they were designed by Frederick Gibberd (architect) and Donavan Lee (engineer). The steel frame for the house and roof was constructed entirely before any cladding was added. Windows were then fixed in position, and finally the buildings were clad, with light pressed-steel sheets being used on the upper half. Most then had a $4\frac{1}{2}$-inch brick skin built to the ground floor. The steel frame remained in a cavity, and the inner part of the wall was of foamed slag and breeze slabs or plasterboard. Metal was used at every opportunity and

148/ British Iron and Steel Federation Houses under construction at Northolt, West London in 1947. Note how the entire structure is erected before any cladding is added. **149/** A 1944 photograph of an early BISF form which had an extra window casement to the type usually seen. **150/** One of the thousands of BISF permanent prefabs that survive in good condition. This example is in rural Yorkshire.

even the ceilings were plaster on expanded metal. 'The design of this house, whilst following English traditions, is extremely able', concluded D Dex Harrison in his 1945 international *Survey of Prefabrication*.

The BISFs were fitted with a newly designed closable fire with back boiler, but there were problems with the flue design (causing several accidental fires), and a 1953 report caused the design to be revised. Two types were produced, the BISF 'A' and BISF 'B'. Essentially similar, the BISF 'B' used a cold-formed rather than a hot-rolled steel frame, and there were minor cladding differences. BISF 'B's had horizontal (rather than vertical) ribbed steel sheeting on the upper half. Some 30,000 were erected, and many remain in good condition.

The Airey House

The Airey concrete home, which came in 'Rural' or 'Urban' varieties, with flat or pitched roofs, was a simple but effective post-and-slab construction produced by William Airey & Sons of Leeds. Further choice was provided in two types, the 'South Aspect' and the 'North Aspect' houses, with the former taking a few more man-hours to construct. Despite costing more than standard brick construction, some 20,000 Airey homes were erected with a Ministry of Works subsidy. Many remain in good condition and are much loved by their residents.

The 1947 handbook for builders of Airey homes recommended a squad of six men, two for fixing the units and four for carrying, holding, assisting, etc. It was estimated that a contractor with no previous experience of the system would be able to erect a pair of Airey houses in 410 man-hours. Posts and slabs were stacked on the ground on all four sides of the concrete foundation, and the walls were built up section by section, the ground floor being completed before the upper storey was attempted. Window frames were aluminium alloy.

151/   152/

The Scottwood

The only truly prefabricated two-storey house was the Scottwood, designed by Hubert Scott-Paine, the founder of the British Power Boat Co. After erecting a successful detached prototype (still standing in Totton), he diverted production of his factory from power boats to semi-detached houses. The external walls and partitions were factory-made timber panels up to 24 feet (7.3 metres) long which were clad in plywood and filled with glass-fibre insulation. The floor and roof had a similar treatment, causing some reservations about a possible fire hazard. London County Council erected some 300 Scottwoods from 1948, giv-

151/ Urban-type Airey house under construction at Chingford in 1946. Being more expensive than traditional brick houses, their construction was subsidised by the Ministry of Works. 152/ Airey house at Aberystwyth in original condition, although its neighbour has been reskinned in traditional brick.

154/

155/

153/ A Scottwood house being erected in Southampton. This photo was taken just eight hours after work began. All ground-floor outside panels, internal partitions, flooring and ceilings are erected. This view illustrates the second-storey panel being lowered into position. 154/ The completed Scottwood House was constructed of laminated wood, providing the strength of a brick-built house, but with only a tenth of the weight. Four men could erect the main structure in a day. 155/ The interior of the Scottwood prototype that appears surprisingly interwar in style considering it was built just after World War 2.

156/

ing them a pitched roof rather than following the proposed flat-roof design. An estate at Morden, London survived into the 1990s, but the lamination on the outer layer of plywood shrank, leaving cracks in the grain.

Other Permanent Prefab Types

Many other partly prefabricated non-traditional houses were erected in post-war Britain, and to describe them all is beyond the scope of this book. Like their interwar predecessors, they can be divided into three categories: steel framework, concrete (precast or poured *in-situ*); and timber (as framework or

156/ Howard Houses at Swindon in 1947. Frederick Gibberd's design in steel and timber could be built as semi-detached pairs (as here) or in long terraces. 157/ The Howard House came with a ready fitted kitchen unit not dissimilar to those fitted in temporary prefabs.

158/ Prototype for the Riley house, November 1946. Although very similar to the BISF prefab, the Riley house was never put into production.

stressed-skin plywood construction). Of the pre-war prefabs only the Boot, Duo-Slab and the Atholl houses continued in production in the post-war period. Some were regionally distinct, such as the post-war Atholl which was only erected in Scotland. Some were only erected by local authorities, but several were privately manufactured and retailed, such as the Cornish Unit. The same factories that had produced the THP prefabs, such as the Orlit, Spooner and Tarrans, manufactured some improved, permanent models.

Many of the new designs were of precast reinforced-concrete (PRC) construction, such as the Unity & Butterley, Wates & Dyke and the Reema Hollow Panel. Several were variants on the BISF model. Others include the Boswell, Braithwaite, Clothed Concrete Constructions, Dorran, Gregory, Howard & Co., Jicwood, Keyhouse Unibuilt, Myton, Newland, Parkinson, PRC, Riley, Smith, Stent, Stonecrete, Timber Development Association, Underdown, Waller, Wessex, Winget and Woolaway.

---

[1] Anthony 1945, page 45.
[2] Diamant 1964, page 7.
[3] See White 1965, pages 166–224, Diamant 1964, Gloag and Wornum 1946, HMSO, 1959 for further reading.
[4] Gloag and Wornum 1946, page 89.
[5] Gloag and Wornum 1946.
[6] See Scottish Executive Building Division 2001 for more on post-war non-traditional building in Scotland. Few of the imported Swedish prefabs in Scotland have survived because of the climate.
[7] See also *RIBA Journal*, August 1939 and *The Architects' Journal*, 7 March 1935.
[8] See also Smart 1999, pages 135–6, who references LCC/MIN 7631, and council minutes of 12 December 1961 and 31 March 1963, all in London Metropolitan Archives, 40 Northampton Road, London EC1R 0HB.

> Permanence comes in the structures of the city, but death comes with it … The permanence of stone and brick, which enables them to defy time, causes them also ultimately to defy life.
>
> *Lewis Mumford*

The THP prefabs were the first and last attempt by the government to provide housing direct to the public. They were a temporary solution designed to represent the better world that people had been told they were fighting for in World War 2, and in virtually every case they satisfied or exceeded the expectations of post-war Britons. Prefabs changed British housing forever.

> Mr J Westwood MP, has told a Glasgow Labour Party housing conference that the kitchen unit in the new 'temporary' dwelling would be the envy of four-fifths of the women in Scotland, and he added … that once the standard of equipment for temporary houses had been set, no Local Authority would dare to put inferior equipment into permanent houses.[1]

Despite their poor insulation, compact size and ineffective heating, prefabs are almost universally admired by their residents, and in many cases the same people who moved into them in 1945–49 remain in their 'temporary' homes. As one Newport resident put it to me, 'When life is this good, why move?' Others have waited for years to be allocated a prefab, turning down any other council accommodation.

159/ Jack Brown, 82, campaigning to save his BL8 resident at Dolphin Road, Redditch, from destruction. After half a century, a move would be 'too much upheaval'.

epilogue/

160/

160/ The garden of this Arcon has been slabbed over for convenience, but the prefab remains a treasured home. 161/ Despite extensive cladding and modernisation, this example is still recognisable as a prefab.

162/

163/

162/ All of the Temporary Housing Programme prefabs were popular with their occupants, many of whom remained in their original prefab until it was demolished. Here Nellie Jones enjoys a cup of tea at her drop-down fitted Arcon kitchen table, just as she has done every day for half a century. 163/ Nellie Jones chats to Stan Carpenter of the Ridgeway Hill estate in Newport. Residents of prefab estates formed close community bonds and they invariably say that friendships with neighbours are what they value most. 164/ After Margaret Thatcher allowed council tenants to buy their own homes, many purchased their prefabs. This example at Newport has since been reskinned in brick and is desperately trying to appear as a bungalow of standard construction.

164/

> I waited 13 years for my prefab. I didn't want any old council house, I wanted a prefab, and I have been here 33 years since. /Mrs South, Bishpool estate, Newport

Some residents even reported that they planned for a second child when the council told them that having just one didn't qualify them for a prefab.

Living in a prefab gave many people a strong sense of identity, and residents proudly rebutted jokes about living in 'Asbestosville' or 'Tin Can Alley'.

> I remember my brother said 'Oh, so you're moving to a chicken shed', and I heard that others said that 'only the scum' live in prefabs, but I didn't care. I was thrilled with my prefab. /Minnie Louvain-Owen, who remains in her Arcon after 53 years

165/

165/ A pantile roof has been added to this Arcon in Newport. 166/ The largest remaining Uni-Seco estate is at Catford in south-east London, protected by Conservation Area status.

166/

Others left their prefab only to find that traditional housing wasn't for them, and then had to wait years on the council housing list to get another prefab. In some cases generations of the same family have all opted to live in prefab homes.

> I used to live in London, but read in a newspaper that a lady in Cardiff wanted to
> exchange her prefab for a London flat, so we proceeded with the exchange.
> I never regretted the move as prefabs are so comfortable, and the housework is
> done in no time. /Joan Dickens

The THP prefabs were less of success story for the government, and when Winston Churchill returned to power as prime minister in 1951, Britain was still short of a million homes. All of the prefab types proved more expensive than had been anticipated, and the experiment demonstrated that factory production of homes didn't save money. The project did provide continued employment in industries that had swollen during the war years, and also gave a very visible indicator that the government was attempting to address the housing shortage.

By the time the last THP prefab was handed over in March 1949 most local authorities had developed plans for permanent publicly owned housing, such as the distinctive, long terraces designed by Tayler and Green for the Loddon Rural District Council in Norfolk (built from 1950 to 1964). Few of the house types that succeeded the prefabs would attract the same admiration from residents; people wanted detached homes with large gardens, and well-designed, light interiors.

> Whoever designed the prefabs originally must have been a very caring and sensible person, in that they are well appointed and ideally placed catching maximum sunlight, an aspect often overlooked by house builders. /Mildred Bowman of the Brynglas estate at Newport

Despite being planned for only a ten- or 15-year life, the great majority of THP prefabs far exceeded this. Although the imported US type seem to have required replacing around 15 years after their erection, many of the hardier types (Arcons, Phoenixes and Uni-Secos) lasted for decades, and some remain in good condition to this day.

> It was in early 1965 that the council informed us that they would be pulling down our prefab estate and building houses on the site. Everybody who lived there was offered the chance of moving back to the houses when they were built, but we

167/ This Uni-Seco at Catford is trying to be a timber-framed country cottage, with replacement 'leaded' cottage windows, a neo-Georgian panelled door and mock timber-frame cladding. The decorative gateposts only add to the charm. 168/ pages 226–227: Derelict Arcons awaiting demolition on the Bishpool estate in Newport.

never did. We were moved to another estate about three miles away. We had been given a council house with a garden, in fact everything that the prefab had, only better … but it wasn't. /Ken Wakefield

In 1975 some 10,000 of the 156,000 THP homes were estimated to be still standing. The majority of those removed in the first 30 years were replaced for reasons other than structural failure. Estates tended to be cleared where land values were greatest, as two houses could often be built on the plot of one prefab. By 1991 fewer than 300 of the 10,000 Greater London prefabs remained (the majority of these being a large estate of Uni-Secos).

Among the reasons that so many prefabs have lasted so long are the

169/ Graffiti begs passers by to 'Save Me' on this boarded-up Newport Arcon awaiting demolition.

valiant campaigns organised by residents to save their homes from demolition. As the years progressed the prefabs lost their uniformity as people individualised their bungalows. This usually started with the introduction of garden statues and trellises, and later, after Margaret Thatcher allowed residents to buy their homes, with the addition of bay windows, leaded-glass lights, and other rustic paraphernalia that allowed them to develop an identity as cottage owners.

At the time of writing the largest concentrations of surviving prefabs are in Bristol/Avonmouth (around 700 of four types over 14 estates), Newport (c. 300 Arcons) and Catford in London (153 Uni-Secos). Many of these homes are under demolition or are threatened with demolition, and Britain's largest and best-preserved estates in Newport are all currently under demolition. Large numbers of permanent prefab types remain, including many BISF homes, and a well-preserved group of LCC mobile homes is to be found by South Bank University, off the Borough Road in London.

The only THP homes to have been afforded the statutory protection of listing are a group of Phoenixes at 394–427 Wake Green Road in Moseley, Birmingham. The Department of Culture, Media and Sport is currently considering a further row of Phoenixes at 38–48 (even nos.) Walton Road, Bristol, but the city council is opposing the listing. A small group of six Arcons, at 75–99 (odd nos.) Blackswarth Road, Bristol is also being considered, and the Catford Uni-Secos are now within a conservation area.

170/

171/

New approaches to prefabrication
Prefabrication of British homes is, if anything, undergoing a renaissance of interest.

> When we first started seriously to think about the prefabricated home, everybody jumped to the conclusion that it would lead to monotony. I say it offers us a way of building truly imaginative and exciting homes. /Richard Rogers

The furniture retailer Ikea is linking up with Swedish developer Skanska to offer affordable prefab housing to the thousands of key workers who can no longer afford to live in London. Ikea has successfully tested the concept, called Bo Klok, or Live Smart, in Sweden, where it is selling prefabricated homes decked out with Ikea furnishings to the lower end of the housing market. Developments in York and by the Peabody Trust in London have also demon-

172/

strated the viability of blocks of flats constructed from prefabricated modular units. Once again the photographers have been out in the streets capturing the impressive moment when instant factory-made homes arrive on the back of lorries. As British house prices continue to rise and exclude more and more people from the property ladder, it seems increasingly likely that there will be yet another call for the palaces for the people.

[1] 'More critics of the Churchill-Portal House', page 132 in *The Architect and Building News*, 2 June 1944.

170/ A replacement bungalow next door to an original Arcon on the Treberth estate in Newport. By 2004 all the original prefabs will have been demolished. **171/** Yorkon prefab housing units being craned into position. The individual units are factory made and arrive ready for construction within the block of flats. **172/** The completed Yorkon prefab flats. The future of prefabrication in Britain?

places to visit/

The only listed THP prefabs are the Phoenixes at 394–427 Wake Green Road, Moseley, Birmingham (illustrated on pages 95 and 98). There is no public access to the interiors. A handful of the striking 1920s prefabs based on the Nissen system (illustrated on page 28) have also been listed. These can be viewed externally at 1–8 Howell Hill, West Camel, Somerset and Goldcroft Road in Yeovil. A further example has been listed in Ealing, West London.

Fortunately, several THP prefabs have been reconstructed in open-air museums across Britain. It is always advisable to telephone in advance to confirm opening arrangements and to check that the prefab is likely to be open.

Museum of Welsh Life, St Fagans, Cardiff CF5 6XB. Telephone 029 2057 3500 or visit www.nmgw.ac.uk (Aluminium Bungalow)

Imperial War Museum Duxford, Cambridgeshire, CB2 4QR. Telephone 01223 835 000 or visit www.iwm.org.uk/duxford/ (Uni-Seco)

Chiltern Open Air Museum, Newland Park, Gorelands Lane, Chalfont St Giles, Buckinghamshire, HP8 4AB. Telephone 01494 871 117 or visit www.coam.org.uk (Universal)

Avoncroft Museum of Buildings, Stoke Heath, Bromsgrove, Worcestershire, B60 4JR. Telephone 01527 831 363 or visit www.avoncroft.org.uk (Mark V Arcon)

Eden Camp Modern History Theme Museum, Malton, North Yorkshire, YO17 6RT. Telephone 01653 697 777 or visit www.edencamp.co.uk (Tarran)

places to visit

A World War 2 Nissen hut formerly used as a hospital has been restored by the Manx Aviation Preservation Society. Visit them at www.maps.iofm.net

A pair of 1920s prefabricated iron prefabs have been reconstructed at The Black Country Living Museum, Tipton Road, Dudley, West Midlands, DY1 4SQ. Telephone 0121 557 9643 or visit www.bclm.co.uk

Ernö Goldfinger's seminal modernist home is owned by the National Trust and open to the public at 2 Willow Road, Hampstead, London NW3 1TH. Telephone 020 7435 6166 or visit www.nationaltrust.org.uk

For those who want to experience prefab life, the Landmark Trust rents Castle Bungalow near Bideford in Devon as a holiday let. This 1920s Boulton & Paul bungalow sleeps up to four people. Visit www.landmarktrust.co.uk or call 01628 825 920. The author is planning to save an Arcon Mark V and restore it on his land in West Wales with an original interior and furnishings. Follow the progress of this project at www.prefabs.co.uk.

Fans of 1940s and 1950s garden ornaments will enjoy the vintage gnomes on display at The Gnome Reserve, West Putford, Bradworthy, Devon EX22 7XE. Telephone 01409 241 435 or visit www.gnomereserve.co.uk

Readers may be interested in joining the Twentieth Century Society, which campaigns to improve knowledge and understanding of twentieth-century architecture. The Society may be contacted at 70 Cowcross Street, London EC1M 6EJ. Telephone 020 7250 3857 or visit www.c20society.org.uk.

Australian readers might like to visit one of Britain's oldest commercially produced prefabs, La Trobe's cottage, that was exported to Melbourne from Britain in 1839. It is owned by the National Trust of Australia and open to the public. Telephone 03 9654 5528 or visit www.nattrust.com.au.

bibliography/

anonymous 1944 'More critics of the Churchill-Portal House', page 132 in *The Architect and Building News*, 2 June

Anthony, H 1945 *Houses. Permanence and Prefabrication*, London: Pleiades Books

Arcon, Chartered Architects 1948 'The design, organisation and production of a prefabricated house' pages 78–80 in *Building* Vol. 23, March

Association of Building Technicians 1946 *Homes for the People*, London: Paul Elek

Bahamon, A 2002 *Prefab. Prefabricated and Moveable Architecture*, New York: Hearst Books International

Baker, P 1991 *Fashions of a Decade – 1940s*, London: B T Batsford

Barrett, H, and J Phillips 1987 *Suburban Style. The British Home 1840–1960*, London: Little Brown & Co.

Batsford, H 1946 *How to See the Country*, London: B T Batsford

Bayley, R 2002 *Celebrating Special Buildings: the Case for Conserving Post-War Public Housing*, London: Twentieth Century Society

BBC 1944 *Homes for All*, Worcester: Littlebury

Bowley, M 1966 *The British Building Industry*, Cambridge: Cambridge University Press

Brown, M, and C Harris 2001 *The Wartime House: Home Life in Wartime Britain 1939–1945*, Stroud: Sutton

Burkhart, B, and A Arieff 2002 *Prefab*, Salt Lake City: Gibbs Smith Publishers

Burnett, J 1986 (2nd edition) *A Social History of Housing 1815–1985*, London: Routledge

Carter, B 1993 *Home Blown: The History of the Homes of Richland*, Richland (USA): The City of Richland

Casson, H 1946 *Homes by the Million: An Account of the Housing Achievement in the USA, 1940–1945*, Harmondsworth: Penguin Books

Columbia River Exhibition undated (1990s) *ABC Homes. The Houses that Hanford Built. A–Z House Plans*, Richland (USA): Columbia River Exhibition

Cook Batsford, B 1987 *The Britain of Brian Cook*, London: B T Batsford

Cox. B H 1945 *Prefabricated Homes*, London: Paul Elek

Council of Industrial Design 1946 *Design '46: Survey of British Industrial Design as displayed at the 'Britain Can Make It' exhibition*, London: HMSO

Diamant, R M E 1964 *Industrialised Building*, London: Iliffe Books (3 vols.)

Denby E 1933 'Women and Kitchens', pages 113–115 in *Design For To-Day* Vol. I, May–December

Denby E 1938 *Europe Re-housed*, London: George Allen & Unwin

Dover, H 1991 *Home Front Furniture: British Utility Design 1941–1951*, Aldershot: Scolar Press

Field, S 1991 *London Prefabs and the Case for Prefabs* [unpublished report]

Finnemore, B 1982 *Aluminium Building: A Study of Post-War Diversification and State Building Policy 1942–1959*, unpublished Masters thesis, University College London

Finnemore, B 1985 'The AIROH house: industrial diversification and state building policy' in *Construction History* Vol.1, pages 60–71

Fetters, T T 2002 *The Lustron Home: The History of a Postwar Prefabricated Housing Experiment*, McFarland & Company

Fairchild, E C (ed.) 1942 *Design for Britain*, London: Dent

Forty, A 1972 'Wireless style: symbolic design and the English radio cabinet 1928–1933', pages 23-31 in *Architectural Association Quarterly* Vol. 4, spring

Forty, A 1986 *Objects of Desire: Design and Society Since 1750*, London: Thames & Hudson

Gay, O 1986 *The Prefab – a Study in Policy-Making*, unpublished MSc thesis, Birkbeck College

Gay, O 1987 'Prefabs: a Study in Policy Making', pages 407–422 in *Public Administration* Vol. 65, winter

Gibb, A 1999 *Off-Site Fabrication: Prefabrication, Pre-assembly and Modularization*, London: John Wiley & Sons

Gloag, J, and G Wornum 1946 *House out of Factory*, London: George Allen & Unwin

Harwood, E 2003 (2nd edition) *England: A Guide to Post-War Listed Buildings*, London: B T Batsford

Harrison, D Dex, J M Albery and M W Whiting 1945 *A Survey of Prefabrication*, London: Ministry of Works

Health, Ministry of 1942 'Memo to the Official Committee on Post-War Internal Economic Problems (IEP) June 1942' in *HLG* 101 377 at Public Record Office, London

Health, Ministry of 1947 *Airey Rural House Handbook of Erection Instructions*, London

Hillier, B 1975 *Austerity/Binge*, London: Studio Vista

HMSO 1959 *A Study of Alternative Methods of House Construction*, National Building Studies, Special Report No. 30

Jackson A 1991 (2nd edition) *Semi-Detached London*, London: Allen & Unwin

Joad, C E M. 1943 *The Adventures of the Young Soldier in Search of the Better World*, London: Faber & Faber

Kendall, N 1971 'The House of 500 Houses in Old Kent Road', pages 106–7 in *House & Garden* XXVI, No. 8, October

Kohan, C M 1952 *Works and Buildings*, London: HMSO

Madge, J (ed.) 1946 *Tomorrow's Houses*, London: Pilot Press

McLaren, G 1997 *Ceramics of the 1950s*, Princes Risborough: Shire

Neel, E 1943 'Tarran System of Construction', page 212 in *Architectural Design and Construction*, October

Patten, M 1990 *We'll Eat Again: A Collection of Recipes from the War Years*, London: Hamlyn

Rankine, A 1942 'A war-time hospital in Hull', *The Builder*, 6 March

Robertson, I H 1947 *Reconstruction and the Home*, London: The Studio

Robins, G 2001 *Prefabrications. Newport's Temporary Bungalows – The First Fifty Years*, Cardiff: Ffotogallery

Ryan, D S 1997 *The Ideal Home Through the 20th Century*, London: Hazar Publishing

Scottish Executive Building Division 2001 (2nd edition) *A Guide to Non-traditional Housing in Scotland*, The Stationery Office Agencies

Short, J R 1982 *The Post-War Experience: Housing in Britain*, London: Methuen

Slater, T 1987 *Batsford's 'Face of Britain': Topographical Writing 1930–1960 and Images of Britain*, Department of Geography, University of Birmingham Working Paper Series No. 37

Smart, A (ed.) 1999 *London Suburb,s* London: Merrell

Sparke, P 1986 *Did Britain Make It?*, London: Design Council

Squire, R 1984 *Portrait of an Architect*, London: Colin Smythe

Stevenson, G 2002 (reprint) *Art Deco Ceramics*, Princes Risborough: Shire

Stevenson, G 2002 (reprint) *The 1930s Home*, Princes Risborough: Shire
Vale, B 1990 *Ideals and Realities: The Temporary Housing Programme*, unpublished PhD thesis, Sheffield University
Vale, B 1995 *Prefabs. A History of the UK Temporary Housing Programme*, London: E & F N Spon
Wallace, D 1946 *How to Grow Food*, London: B T Batsford
White, R B 1965 *Prefabrication. A History of Its Development in Great Britain* London: HMSO
Wood, M 1989 *'We wore what we'd got': Women's Clothes in World War II*, Devon: Wheaton
Works, Ministry of 1942 'Note by Ernest Simon of the Ministry of Works 5.3.42' in *CAB 123 123* at the Public Record Office, London
Works, Ministry of 1948 *Temporary Housing Programme*, Cmd. 7304 London: HMSO

picture credits/

I am grateful to photographers Elisabeth Blanchet, Peter Cuffley, Robert Drake, Shirley Gibbs, Rob Hadden, Kate Jones, Alan Mason, Richard Page, Gary Robins and Andy Wilkinson for permission to reproduce their images, and also the dozens of prefab dwellers who allowed me to borrow their wonderful family photographs.

National Monuments Record: pictures 7, 13, 14, 15, 16, 21, 22, 23, 25, 26, 27, 28, 30, 34, 35, 39, 46, 48, 49, 50, 51, 53, 54, 56, 57, 58, 60, 63, 64, 65, 66, 71, 72, 73, 74, 78, 136, 138, 139, 140, 141, 142, 143, 144, 148, 149, 151, 156, 157, 156; The Imperial War Museum: pictures 18, 19, 20, 108, 115; The Museum of Welsh Life: pictures 59, 61, 62, 75, 110, 123, 124; The Geffrye Museum: pictures 83, 84, 119; The Black Country Living Museum: picture 5; The Landmark Trust: picture 6; Croydon Local Studies Library: picture 38; Barking & Dagenham Library Services: picture 47; Southampton County Council Cultural Services: pictures 77, 137, 153, 154, 155; Yorkon: pictures 171, 172; Punch Magazine: picture 17; Amgueddfa Ceredigion: picture 118. The Gnome Reserve, Devon provided the gnome photographs on pages 2 and 234.

All reasonable efforts have been made to trace the copyright holders of the images reproduced in this book. If we were unable to reach you, please contact B T Batsford at the address on page 5.